Sixty Years of British Mus

SIXTY YEARS OF BRITISH MUSIC HALL

John M. Garrett

CHAPPELL & COMPANY
in association with
ANDRÉ DEUTSCH

Chappell & Company Limited
50 New Bond Street, London W1A 2BR

London Amsterdam Brussels Hamburg
Johannesburg Madrid Milan Paris
Stockholm Sydney Toronto Wellington
Zurich New York

First published 1976

Designed by Norman Ball

Printed in Great Britain by
Lowe & Brydone Printers Limited, Thetford, Norfolk
Production in association with
Book Production Consultants, Cambridge

ISBN 0 903443 13 9

To JOY

for her tireless assistance

AND

To PETER HONRI

*for his friendship and for rekindling
my enthusiasm for this book*

CONTENTS

I should like to acknowledge my gratitude to the various sources of information, books, historians, collectors, radio programmes, etc which have assisted me in the preparation of this book. I would especially like to thank Mr Peter Honri, the Ascherberg Archives, the Public Records Office, and the following publications:—

Marie Lloyd and Music Hall by Daniel Farson (Tom Stacey Ltd)
Victorian Sheet Music Covers by Ronald Pearsall (David & Charles)
George Robey by Peter Cotes (Cassell)
The British Music Hall by Peter Davison (Oak Publications)
Winkles and Champagne by M. Willson Disher (Cedric Chivers)
Your Own, Your Very Own by Peter Gammond (Ian Allan)
The British Music Hall by Mander & Mitchenson (Studio Vista)

1. Overture

If there is one art form to which Britain can justly and proudly claim to have given birth, it is the music hall. A living entity of boundless vitality, it was a child of dubious parentage, whose father was the drawing-room ballad – the soirée motto song – the nationalistic air, and whose mother was the folk tune – the raucous carouse – the tender love song. This *enfant terrible* had all the disadvantages of being born on the wrong side of the blanket, yet despite this, and perhaps even because of this, it thrived upon the sentiments of every stratum of society in an age when Britain was awakening to the realization of Empire. The infant music hall had but one watchword – 'flamboyance' – fired by an innocent, and as yet uninhibited, passion.

This strange fusion of characteristics arose from the late 1840s in the Cyder Cellars and other low-class drinking places where entertainment was provided. Singers of folk songs, broadsiders and street musicians frequented these establishments where it was common practice for songwriters to hawk their own song sheets: indeed, by 1861 it was estimated that there were no less than 700 ballad singers plying their trade in London alone. Their songs included some which have recently been successfuly revived ('Hard times of old England', 'All around my hat', etc) and these expressed their way of life, their conventions and their outlook upon the world in general. Because of their growing popularity and the clientele they attracted, the tavern managers went to the expense of improving their premises, and by doing so, the emphasis was shifted from the provision of a place of refreshment with entertainment to a place of entertainment with refreshment.

The Georgian coffee houses, which were their direct forerunners, encouraged the formation of small singing groups or 'glee clubs' and by the 1830s song and supper rooms had become favourite meeting-places for the local populace. Evans (late Joys) at 43 King Street, Covent Garden was the most prominent and led to the setting up of tavern music halls such as the Coal Hole in the Strand. From this shift in emphasis, certain artistes became well-known outside their home localities; the first of these being W. G. Ross whose most memorable contribution to the music hall repertoire was the ballad of 'Sam Hall' – a chimney-sweep who was hanged for murder still defiantly cursing 'Damn yer eyes!' as the trap opened. This song was taken up by Sam Cowell who progressed to purveying his own songs, some of which were still popular in later years (his 'Ratcatcher's Daughter' sold over 228 000 copies – a huge sale for those times). Folk songs remained in vogue despite new variants and parodies being written and performed and the example of 'Villikins and his Dinah', a cockney ballad whose melodic roots are lost in the mists of the seventeenth century, still holds audiences today in its quaint innocence and its melodramatic dénouement.

(SPOKEN) *Now this is the most melancholy part of it, and shows what the progeny was druv to in conskivence of the mangled obstropolosness and ferocity of the inconsiderable parient . . .*

(SUNG)	*Now as Villikins was a-walking the garding all around . . .*
(SPOKEN)	*It was the back garding this time*
(SUNG)	*He spied his dear Dinah lying dead on the ground,*
	With a cup of cold pizen all down by her side
	And a billey-dow which said as 'ow 'twas by pizen she died.
(SPOKEN)	*The label was marked 'British Brandy'*
(SUNG)	*Singin' Too-ra-li, too-ra-li, too-ra-li-da.*

It is to be noticed that even in these early stages of music hall tradition, the artiste's patter was included in the song sheets: it gives a good insight into the type of stage routine used at the time.

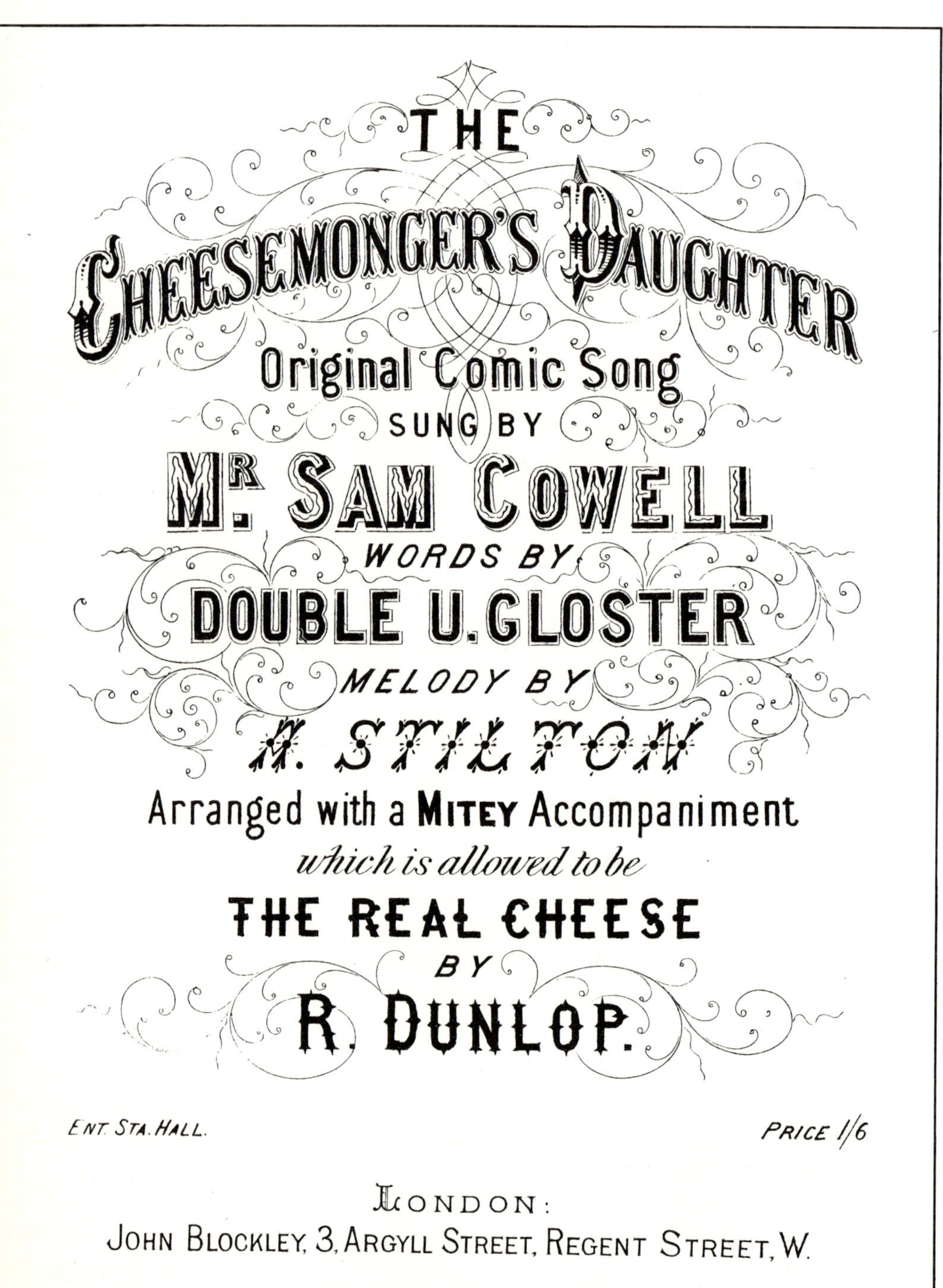

If Anglo-Saxon culture were whittled down to its lowest common denominators, one would probably find a pun, a rude noise and a defiant gesture. The pun was certainly the most used prop of a music hall artiste and indeed remains so to this present day – the more outrageous the pun, the better! A good instance is the early song cover of another Sam Cowell ditty 'The Cheesemonger's Daughter' – and that is only the cover!

Other artistes at this time included Charles Sloman and Jack Sharp - the latter being a comic vocalist whose metier was cockney songs and who, despite his acclaim, died at a Dover workhouse in 1856 aged thirty-eight – a tragic death which was to be all too often repeated by many a music hall artiste thereafter.

Meanwhile the structure of the halls had been changing in their design and convention – accommodating larger audiences and allowing admittance to women, albeit on special nights only. At the outset of the song and supper clubs, the manager had acted as chairman, keeping order and announcing the performers, but now these two operations became too onerous for one person and so a separate position of chairman was created. A raised stage for performers came into common use and areas were even set aside for small groups of musicians.

For the first half of the nineteenth century, the salon singer was a sophisticated breed of artiste who visited the Victorian middle- and upper-class houses and after supper, surrounded by the family and guests, would perform songs of moral uplift and act out harmless little comedies of affluent society. Young ladies of the household would play the piano and accompany themselves and others in ditties of unrequited love and of propriety in Victorian social circles. Yet owing to the growing prosperity and popularity of the music hall with its portrayals of otherwise unnoticed working-class customs and ways of life, its influence percolated through to the 'Upper Ten's' entertainments, and innovations in style and performance crept in from below stairs.

The young music hall received a further boost under the Theatre Act of 1843, which removed the monopoly of drama from the 'legitimate' theatre and gave to the tavern music halls the choice of becoming either a theatre with a dramatic licence from the Lord Chamberlain but without the privilege of selling alcohol in the auditorium, or a tavern concert room with a drinking licence but without the right to produce stage plays. Most tavern music halls took up the latter option. There was however, a sting in the tail of this Act – the Lord Chamberlain's office now had the right to approve or veto every lyric, monologue and script used in the music halls and this led to many skirmishes between artistes and the law thereafter.

The youthful music hall was growing up fast into a strong, robust adolescent and Charles Morton took upon himself the responsibility of its development *in loco parentis:* not by chance has he become known as 'The Father of the Halls' – he built the Canterbury Hall at the rear of the Canterbury Arms Tavern in Pimlico and this was opened on 17 May 1852. Because of the increased demand, he had the hall lengthened and enlarged and it was reopened on 21 December 1856. The 'Canterbury' was the first formalized music hall as we have come to understand the term. Artistes earned a guinea a week plus their supper every evening and Morton was instrumental in acquiring local artistes from the Cyder Cellars, and elsewhere and placing them at the 'Canterbury' to attract custom from further afield. It was he who encouraged the use of the prefix 'great' for his performers and one of the first to 'come over' from the drawing-room circuit was Harry Clifton, who went down well with his newly-acquired audiences in spite of his singing such middle-class motto songs as 'Work boys, work, and be contented'. His audiences joined in the choruses of many of his motto songs of which 'Paddle your own canoe' is typical. Most of his songs had the underlying inference that it was every Briton's duty to work hard and keep a smiling countenance.

Then love your neighbour as yourself
As the world you go travelling through
And never sit down with a tear or a frown
But paddle your own canoe.

Charles Morton followed up his success at the 'Canterbury' by catering to the demands for this new entertainment in the provinces – he opened numerous music halls outside London and organized tour circuits for his artistes. Other proprietors jumped on the Morton bandwagon and by the mid-1860s there were well over 300 registered music halls on the British mainland. Of course, prominent artistes now could command anything up to £30 or £40 a week and in some cases even more. From the ranks of the song-writer-artistes the first theatrical agent arrived on the scene – his name, George Ware. His agency duties entailed, among other things, writing suitable songs for his clients, including the immortal 'The boy I love is up in the gallery'.

The music hall had come of age and began challenging authority in every shape and form – even the 'Mother of Parliaments': the adolescent youth had given way to the crusading gallant who in turn fostered 'The Great Ones' – 'The Lion Comiques'.

The first of these Victorian trend-setters of culture and fashion was George Leybourne who, by his stylish mannerisms and his vivid characterizations, attracted huge audiences wherever he played. He was the original 'Champagne Charlie' – the epitome of the 'heavy swell', complete with swagger-cane (or 'crutch') and over-correct evening dress. 'George', as he was known to close friends and audiences alike, was the first 'superstar' and earned over £100 per week (an incredible sum for those times). The theatre management supplied him with his own carriage and four white horses so that he could drive between engagements in a style suited to his stage image. He had a melodious voice and could perform his 'business' with a modicum of apparent effort, laying emphasis on a casual wink, a knowing look, or slight stress or pause in what would otherwise seem a quite mundane lyric. In 'Father says I may' one can guess what sly embellishments Leybourne added (the Lord Chamberlain could not censure what audiences thought!):

When I was courting Nellie Clair
I often used to say,
'Whatever you think of doing, love,
Ask father if you may.'

Whatever she might wish for, I
Of course could ne'er refuse
So the darling did just as she pleased
For this was her excuse:

CHORUS: *Father says I may, Georgie, father says I may,*
Of course you can't say 'no', Georgie, if father says I may,
Father says I may, Georgie, father says I may
So don't say 'no' for it is no 'go', since father says I may.

Following hard on Leybourne's heels came Alfred Vance who preferred to be known as 'The Great Vance'. Unlike Leybourne, he was originally a straight actor but he turned to music hall capitalizing on his boyish good looks and charm to become one of the early female impersonators. He later took up the rich man-about-town image in the wake of Leybourne's success in this role.

The third member of the Lion Comiques trio was G. H. Macdermott who in some ways went on to eclipse the other two in popularity and style: although he did not have the singing voice of Leybourne and did not attempt characterization to such an extent as Vance, he could hold an audience and twist them around his finger. He too had been primarily an actor but went on to become the first of the trio to work his acts purely in evening dress without any costume changes.

The Lion Comiques in fact were artistes who appeared larger than life, and whose popular power was felt, with not a little trepidation, by politician and Establishment alike: it came to such a pass that one could almost see an MP visibly look over his shoulder before making an important speech or taking a policy decision. These 'Great Ones' were the nineteenth century ombudsmen – the people's spokesmen on every aspect of the British way of life, and it was through their influence that the music hall ballad steered a course away from the traditional folk form to that of contemporary social comment: the 'pop' songs of their day. These covered a wealth of topics and reflected the varied and knowledgeable interests of the audience (while showing up the popular inbred suspicions of anything that they, the audiences, did not understand).

The police force came in for a lot of humorous criticism in this manner, as did any representative of authority. Freemasonry was acquiring an enthusiastic following at this time, claiming to be the panacea for all society's ills and so Macdermott pricked its balloon of self-importance with 'Give me a grip of your hand', exploiting the underlying suspicion of its secret rituals. Through the astounding manifestations of Daniel Dunglas Home, spiritualism became the centre of attraction in middle-class back parlours and this also did not escape the attentive Macdermott: from 'Rap, rap, rap, I'm married to a medium':

One day my wife an eel pie made, her hand at crust was light,
And when that pie was opened, I beheld a pretty sight,
The eels, tho' baked, were spirit *eels, and in their skins so sable*
They wriggled out and danced about, like scorpions on the table . . .
(SPOKEN) *. . . and the knives, and forks, the plates and dishes, the glasses,*
the cruet stand – all began to bob up and down with a –
(CHORUS) *Rap, Rap, Rap, I'm married to a medium . . .*

Drinking ditties were ever a favourite entertainment of the halls (after all, they did originate from tavern audiences). Leybourne and Vance fought a running battle of repartee singing about various kinds of beverage: Leybourne sang 'Champagne Charlie' – Vance retorted with 'Cool Burgundy Ben' – there followed 'Moet & Chandon', 'Sparkling Moselle', 'Clicquot' and so on down through the wine list eventually culminating with Vance's 'Beer!'.

Aspects of married life were always fruitful Aunt Sallys for the music hall singer along with parodied and over-hammed temperance ballads: they supplied the working-class audiences with cameos of domesticity with which they could identify:

I loved a girl as fair as coal –
Her Christian name was Mary –
When I kissed her she shed three of her teeth
*Then I threw her down an area . . .**
. . . I had a hated rival! – yes
One ninety-five years young:
I bravely stabbed him in the rear
For which sweet Mary swung (just because I loved her).

About the mid 1880s, decimalization and the twenty-four hour clock had been discussed in Parliament. We have to thank the former for the florin, and the latter for this next gem of outrageous logic for future legislation:

At two foot six, I hope you'll call and take a five foot tea,
I hope you'll spare an inch or two to come and chat with me,
At twenty feet past fourteen miles, we'll sit and wonder how
The clock strikes rods and feet and where the devil are we now?

Other forms of entertainment gave rise to music hall skits – Leybourne's 'The daring young man on the flying trapeze' was written in honour of Léotard's act at the Alhambra, and his 'The belle of the rink' commemorated the craze of roller-skating in the late 1860s (Waldteufel's 'Skaters' Waltz' was also written in celebration of this pastime).

Protest songs were always reliable vehicles for music hall entertainers (they could count on at least half the audience agreeing with their point of view and gaining the remainder's acquiescence merely by their stage presence). G. W. Hunt's 'We don't want to fight but by jingo, if we do' provided Macdermott with a truly rousing patriotic song at the time of the Russo-Turkish War in 1877 – it also provided Hunt with a nickname and the English language with a new word 'Jingoism'. Had Palmerston with his 'Gunboat' diplomacy been alive, and had he the backing of Messrs Hunt and Macdermott, there is little doubt that, to a man, their audiences would have trooped out to war without a moment's hesitation.

We don't want to fight, but by jingo if we do
We've got the ships, we've got the men, and got the money too,
We've fought the Bear before, and while we're Britons true,
The Russians shall not have Constantinople.

Animals have always found a soft spot in the hearts of Englishmen and so

*A sunken court in front of a basement of a house or tenement.

it was in 1882 when the London Zoo sold their bull elephant 'Jumbo' to Barnum's Circus for £2000: it provoked a storm of criticism, questions in the House and even more protest songs: 'Why part with Jumbo (the pet of the Zoo)'. The protest was of no avail but Jumbo obviously did not like his new home in America, for in a tantrum, he died venting his anger on a steam locomotive – however, he bequeathed his name to the English language.

In those halcyon days of the British Empire, when the Lion Comiques were at the peak of their power, when the music halls were bustling with the clamour and boom of business, and when Parliament was the focal point

of the world, political scandal and gossip were rife. When, in 1885, a highly promising politician named Dilke was involved in the 'three in a bed' divorce scandal, the result was a ruined career and another successful song for 'The Great Macdermott' – 'Master Dilke upset the milk when taking it home to Chelsea'. (Such was the Victorian's powerful illusion of his superior morals, that in 1890, another divorce case cited Charles Parnell and, by mere implication, ruined the standing of a man who might have settled 'the Irish Question' once and for all.)

Another affront to the Victorians' respectability in the 1880s arose from the exposure of the activities of certain titled gentlemen at a London night-spot which resulted in Labouchere's 'Homosexual Bill': this topic was subtly remarked upon in 'Fishing for Truth in a well' and it is possible that we have absorbed the modern colloquialism from the last line of this quotation:

Fishing for Truth in a well,
Some wonderful things she will tell,
Our friend Labouchere went angling there
And caught some queer fish in the well.

With the waning of the Lion Comiques' power, the Lord Chamberlain exerted more control on music hall artistes and never again were his instructions flouted with such impunity. All the time that the Lion Comiques had held sway, many imitators in style and material made their names on the music hall circuits and were known as 'Minor Lions'. The music hall was now slowly but inexorably approaching middle age and a new generation of artistes was emerging – female serios and male impersonators, such as Vesta Tilley, were becoming acceptable to a new generation of audiences, especially after the deaths of Vance and Leybourne, and Macdermott's retirement. Jugglers, ventriloquists, black-faced minstrels and other novelty acts took up a greater proportion of the billing.

During this time the music hall premises too had undergone alteration: the early buildings had been reconstructions and makeshift annexes for audience and performers, but by the 1870s new halls, *per se*, had been built with a stage, movable scenery, orchestra pit, and adequate audience facilities. New regulations were enacted so that drinking salons were separated from the auditoria, and after numerous fires up and down the country, iron safety curtains were required by the 'Certificate of Safety' law of 1878. Safety licences were issued annually by the Metropolitan Board of Works (for city areas) and, due to the strict enforcement of this law by their inspectors, many unsafe music halls were closed down (including some well-known and well-loved ones such as Wilton's).

The spirit of the music hall was diversifying into offshoots of other musical entertainment. In the late 1870s Augustus Harris imported comedians and serio-comics from the halls and presented a new style of Christmas production called 'Pantomime'; these founded the traditions of a dame played by a man in woman's dress and a female principal boy. From the background of the Gilbert and Sullivan operettas came a new impressario – George Edwardes. He put on productions at the Gaiety Theatre in the 1890s which went under the name of musical comedies and these revived the ebullient atmosphere of the music hall adding the splendour of lavish presentation – Edwardes could be described as the precursor of Busby Berkeley, for he gave the West End stage what Berkeley later brought to Hollywood.

Oswald Stoll created rival revues at the London Coliseum – his productions were always within 'good taste' for Stoll himself watched and vetted every act. Both Edwardes' and Stoll's examples were copied by other smaller theatres and, against this background of lavish presentation, the music hall became self-conscious and inhibited: from this it was never to recover.

With the new influences in music ('Coon songs' and later 'Ragtime'), the Vaudeville acts from America, and the introduction of the bioscope into many theatres, the British character of music hall became diluted. The conglomerate heading for this commonwealth of entertainment was 'Variety', yet even with the introduction of various Royal Command Performances which set the social seal on music hall, the old charisma could not be resurrected. One of the reasons for this lay in the fact that Variety productions took on the mantle of middle-class mores and as such, deterred the working classes from hearing and seeing artistes with whom they could more readily identify. The outstanding omission on the bill of every Royal Variety Performance was Marie Lloyd, who, to prove her popularity, ran a rival presentation called 'The People's Command'.

On 18 February 1906, the Variety Artistes Federation (the music hall's trade union) was founded; it was set up to further the interests of the music hall artistes who in general had had a very raw deal from the theatre management – their working conditions and wages were poor. Their demands conflicted with the hall proprietors' interests and in 1907 it came to a head when the VAF called a strike. Their basic demands were for recognition of their union, improvements in working conditions and set scales and rates for certain performances and billing. The strike lasted a month enforced by fierce picketing and eventually the proprietors ceded to the VAF's demands; it was many more years, however, before all the requirements were fully met.

Variety continued without further major changes right up to the First World War when the first realization of mechanized warfare and its horrors brought about a sobering change of attitude in the populace and thence into the theatre. The disruptive influence of the bioscope developed into a positive threat with the consolidation of the cinema and its attendant establishments. The era of musical comedy had passed and was now superseded by revue. During the war many of these were staged throughout theatres nationally and the *esprit* of an ailing music hall was temporarily revived by the patriotism inherent in marching songs such as 'It's a long way to Tipperary': but, by the end of the war, the euphoria of victory quickly gave way to the feeling of disappointment and then resentment at finding no 'land fit for heroes'.

The early twenties were a time of growing unemployment, the birth of radio and the burgeoning of the silent movie and the gramophone – all of which did not help the cause of the music hall: the few who had the money visited the picture palace in preference to the music hall, and those who did not have any money could not afford the music hall, thus breaking the last fragile link in the chain which constituted its social origins.

With the introduction of 'talkies', cinemas became luxurious in the extreme and their prices remained lower than those of the live theatre. Radio and gramophone records attracted the more well-known names in Variety and it is probable that had the Second World War not come about, the death-throes of music hall would have come sooner. The 1939–45 war brought about yet another recovery of music hall-type entertainment, but this time in programme format over the radio. ENSA was formed and its artistes toured all over the world giving morale-boosting concerts to the troops.

After the war, revue made a comeback and with radio, television and films, soon undermined the music hall and with the decline of interest in live Variety (in preference for entertainment obtained by the turn of a knob), many great theatres became empty and derelict – most were pulled down in the post-war development schemes. A few survived, however, but were redeployed – the Shepherd's Bush Empire became the BBC TV Studios. The death-rattle of the music hall was finally heard amongst the crash of falling masonry in 1963 when the Metropolitan was demolished to make way for the flyover at Harrow Road. (By a strange quirk of fate, it was decreed that as music hall finally died, two of the basic elements of the young music hall, satire and folk song, were making a startling comeback throughout the world media.)

This then was the music hall – an establishment whose essence and life blood was its 'British-ness' – its rampant nationalism and devil-may-care attitudes. It came in with the accession of a great queen, it reached its prime at the pinnacle of Imperial power and aged visibly with the death of its great monarch, whence it lost momentum and direction and died of neglect.

In this book we remember the years of its youth – its bracing atmosphere, its glorious exuberance, its vulgarity, panache and sentimentality – 'Sixty Years of British Music Hall'.

2. ... And Beginners

Back in those early days of the halls, the only ballad-mongers catering for tavern audiences were the composer-artistes themselves: 'reputable' music publishers would not demean themselves by printing for this market, and dealt only in the salon ballad and the classical and semi-classical keyboard works. Printing costs were prohibitive and customers had to pay four shillings or thereabouts per song copy: some publishers even sent their music to Germany for printing, saving as much as a third of their costs, for it was in Germany that the process of lithography – printing from stone – had been discovered and developed. The principles were evolved by Aloys Senefelder (1771–1834) who, because of the high cost of copper printing plates, had searched for a substitute and had stumbled upon the medium of calcareous limestone. His idea was based on two facts – grease repels water, and calcareous limestone will accommodate both grease and water. Thus, with a piece of paper greased on the underside, one could trace a drawing on to the stone. This could then be washed down with water which would be absorbed by the stone, except for those areas already greased. An ink roller could then be applied to the surface of the stone, the ink adhering to the grease, so that when pressed on to paper, a true copy of the original sketch would be produced.

Despite this innovation, however, music publishers still had to bear the cost of engraving the music, and thus they were not too concerned about printing lavish designs, which resulted in the music covers of the 1830s and 40s resembling title pages of books. It was due to most middle- and upper-class households boasting a piano that the demand for song editions with piano accompaniment was met by publishers, and we have the soirée society to thank for the sheet music format as we know it today. Early song editions were primitive four-sided sheets, closely printed for economy, and the first pictorial covers were introduced in the late 1830s utilizing the top half of the page. Some time elapsed, however, before the 'reputable' publishers appreciated the commercial potential of the music cover, and it took the growth of the music hall ballads to make them see the light. One of the most important factors in the exploitation of the music cover was the development of chromolithography (colour lithography) patented by Engelmann in 1837: this process consisted of using a different stone for each colour required. There were many problems of overlapping arising from printing one colour over another, and it was a good craftsman indeed who could produce a multi-colour picture with fine 'registration'. In the early stages of the colour printing of music covers, fewer colours and therefore fewer stones were used – on 'Polly Perkins of Paddington Green' for instance, the colouring was black and buff on white.

During the formative years of the music hall, many composer-artistes went into business as music publishers, some wheeling and dealing from barrows while others acquired more permanent shop premises. This led to a snowball situation where music halls promoted the sale of songs which in turn promoted the music halls. In the wake of this development, gentlemen 'entrepreneurs' arrived on the scene, visiting both music halls and salon parties and acquiring works from composers in both social environments. In the 1850s when the 'Canterbury' was beginning to flourish, two such gentlemen, William Hopwood and George Crew, founded a music publishing company – Hopwood & Crew. They were lucky, or perhaps very shrewd, for in cultivating songwriter-artistes such as Harry Clifton, they assured themselves of success in future years when he transferred from the salon circuit to the music hall. Another of their protégés was Charles Coote, Jr – a composer who hailed from a middle-class musical background – his father, Charles Coote, Snr (1809–1880) being well-known as a semi-classical composer. His son, however, wrote in lighter vein and his piano pieces became very popular, especially his waltzes and polkas – Harry Clifton even borrowed his melodic themes for the basis of some of his songs. On a broader scale, this interspersal process guaranteed the success of salon pieces in the music hall and vice versa.

Other publishers who set up in business in the 1850s included Charles Sheard, at 148 High Holborn, London, WC and John Blockley (born 1801), a prolific composer of drawing-room ballads (none of which have lasted in popularity). He had many successes with other publishers before starting his own business at 3 Argyll Street, London, W, and understandably the early acquisitions to his catalogue were salon pieces: yet it was by chance that in 1864, one of his agents, John Cameron, bought outright the Sam Cowell copyrights from Morison Kyle – a Scottish music seller at 108 Queen Street, Glasgow. (Morison Kyle was also a part-time agent for Sam Cowell, Arthur Lloyd – before he migrated to the London music halls – and even Arthur Lloyd's father, who was a popular attraction in Scottish halls.)

Blockley also 'picked up' the copyright to 'Villikins and his Dinah' – a song which at the time was suffering a temporary lull in popularity after its hectic twenty years of existence – and with this, and the Sam Cowell songs, Blockley expanded into music hall by acquiring the works of Harry Liston: although his company now had a share of the music hall trade, he still maintained the lucrative salon ballad aspect of his operations.

In the late 1850s full-page colour picture covers became commonplace, especially when publishers realized that a music cover would fit almost exactly into the pane of a shop window. The illustrators of these early covers were paid about £5 to £10 per drawing – many were graduates from newspapers or periodicals. One such was Alfred Concanen who went on to become the foremost cover illustrator of the music hall period: he was born in London in 1835 and his appearance ironically palely mirrored that of the Lion Comique whom he was to immortalize in print. Early in his career, he was a staff illustrator for the *Illustrated Sporting and Dramatic News*, working mainly on sketches drawn from photographs: he married in 1858 and in that year moved to studios in Frith Street, becoming a free-lance artist. Here he designed posters, book illustrations and began his successful rise to fame as a cover artist. For a while he collaborated with a lesser-known artist, Thomas Lee – Concanen being

responsible for the overall design and Lee concentrating on the calligraphy and ornamentation. Concanen worked directly on stone and quickly mastered its intricacies: he was associated with the most prominent lithographic printers of the time – Stannard & Dixon – later Stannard & Son. However, Concanen was not a mere sketcher – he could have passed for a great artist if his living standards had not depended so much on earning commercial commissions. The artwork on the cover of 'Did you ever, no I never' demonstrates this point well for, with fine attention to detail added to a witty perception, he manages to include most of the absurdities mentioned in the song's lyrics – the Scotsman dancing a fling on the top of the omnibus, policemen carrying parasols, the toff wearing his shirt over his jacket and his socks over his boots, and the man with two wooden legs holding a pair of roller-skates. To this he adds an advertisement for another Hopwood & Crew publication – Charles Coote's 'Messenger of Love Waltz' – on the side of the omnibus, while surreptitiously giving the song's publication date in the form of the cabby's registration number: for an encore, he depicts the policemen as having boots many sizes larger than any other person's in the drawing and, for sheer artistry, just look at the astonished expression on the dog in the bottom left-hand corner!

Apart from Concanen, the other 'giant' in the cover illustration field was Alfred Bryan, whose trade-marks were his character studies with large heads and small bodies, accompanied by his initials 'A.B.'. He may well have known Concanen because he too worked for a time on the staff of the *Illustrated Sporting and Dramatic News* – the immediacy and topicality of his journalistic background spilling over into the verve of his sketches. He contributed to many magazines and books and was resident artist for many years to the music hall's own periodical – *The Entr'acte*.

By the 1860s when the Lion Comiques were the rage, just a picture of these 'Great Ones' would be enough to sell a song: many achieved sales of over 10 000 copies. Those of the upper classes, whose self-imposed moral fortitude barred them from visiting the music hall establishments, were not loathe to purchase music hall songs: from the cover likenesses of the superstar trend-setters, they could catch up with all the latest fashions and, one suspects that underneath their strict Victorian façade, they harboured a sneaking admiration for the catchy tunes and the incisive wit of the topical ballads.

At this time there were at least seventy music shops in London alone accommodating the growing demand for music hall songs: many publishers employed travellers who would follow the idols of the day around from theatre to theatre encouraging sales of their latest song. It is probably this way that Messrs Hopwood & Crew encountered George Leybourne, Alfred Vance and G. W. Hunt – Hunt probably introducing them to G. H. Macdermott.

Most of the songs that publishers acquired were bought outright from the composers for a lump sum of anything between one guinea and £10 per song – the publishers submitting these works to the artistes for approval. If they liked and performed these works, the publisher would have the music on sale within the week: this was achieved by preparing the music plates and lithography in advance – even before the artiste had given the first performance of the song!

Upon publication the publisher, to protect his copyright, was under obligation to register his work at Stationers' Hall: the Literary Copyright Act of 1842 required copies to be lodged at the British Museum and certain other libraries and institutions, but failure to do so did not imperil the copyright – however, although registration at Stationers' Hall was not compulsory, it was necessary before any action could be brought against copyright infringers: therefore most publishers registered their works automatically upon publication. The requirement for all published works to be registered at the British Museum for copyright recognition only came about under the 1911 Copyright Act although most publishers up to that date had been doing so as a matter of course.

One of the Lord Chamberlain's licences issued to theatres and music halls.

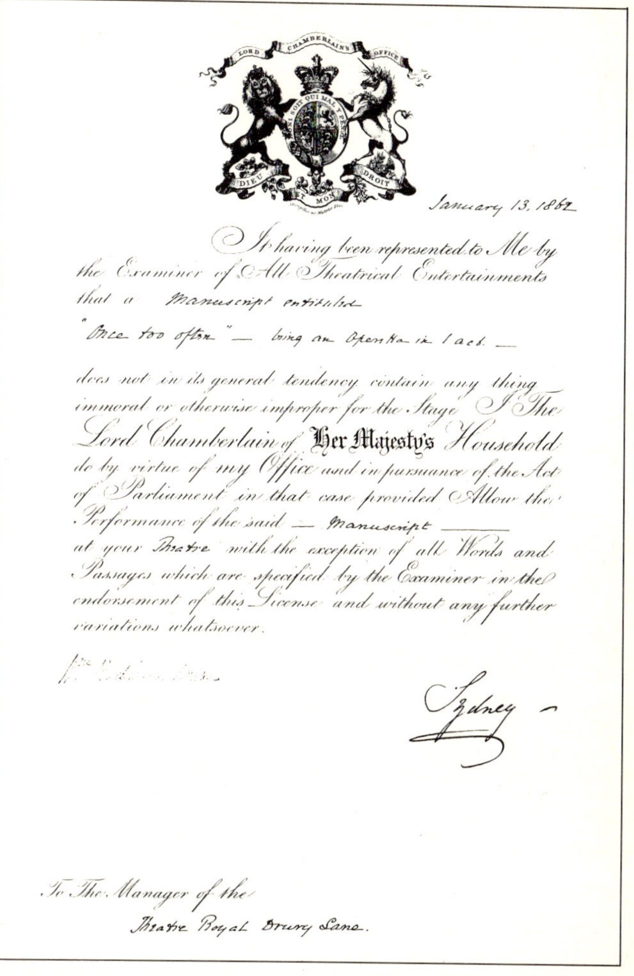

LORD CHAMBERLAIN'S OFFICE

HONI SOIT QUI MAL Y PENSE

DIEU ET MON DROIT

January 13, 1862

It having been represented to Me by the Examiner of All Theatrical Entertainments that a Manuscript entitled "Once too often" — being an Operetta in 1 act. — does not in its general tendency contain any thing immoral or otherwise improper for the Stage I The Lord Chamberlain of Her Majesty's Household do by virtue of my Office and in pursuance of the Act of Parliament in that case provided Allow the Performance of the said — Manuscript — at your Theatre with the exception of all Words and Passages which are specified by the Examiner in the endorsement of this License and without any further variations whatsoever.

Sydney

To The Manager of the Theatre Royal Drury Lane.

Once a song had become successful, the publisher had the problem of marketing this highly-priced music – he overcame this by slashing the marked price by half, thus encouraging greater sales and thereby recouping the balance of the marked down price.

As music hall publications tended to be direct lyrical replicas of the songs and patter of the artiste, the publishers ran the risk of a clash with the Lord Chamberlain – some songs were hastily withdrawn or amended to avoid 'offending public morals'.

On 11 August 1874, William Hopwood died aged forty-three, and early in 1875 George Crew retired from music publishing, surrendering his name and goodwill to the purchase of Charles Coote, Jr and Edward Chappell (nephew of Thomas Patey Chappell of Chappell & Co). The new proprietors concentrated all their efforts into promoting music hall material, and their first success quickly appeared – it was 'Gold, Gold, Gold!', published in March 1875 and still selling twenty-five years later!

Gold, Gold, Gold! I love to hear it jingle,
Gold, Gold, Gold! its power is untold,
We men strive hard to store it
And woman she'll adore it,
The best friend that a man can have is Gold, Gold, Gold!

This song was written by G. W. Hunt but, unlike his predecessors, he did not put his name to the copyright assignment until August that year – he probably held out for better terms over the intervening months as the sales of his song rose higher and higher. In fact it was because of the song's popularity that he received a consideration of one guinea for each hundred copies sold – one of the first instances of a music hall writer receiving a royalty payment: a trend that has been continued and amplified from that time to the present day.

London 3d. July 1875

Received of CHARLES COOTE, JUNR. & EDWARD CHAPPELL, (carrying on business under the Firm of Hopwood and Crew) one copy (value one shilling) for the absolute Sale of all my Copyright and Interest, present and future, vested and contingent, together with the right of representation of and in the Ballad entitled "Faithful ever" words written by me & music composed by Mr. J. L. Hatton under condition of the payment to me of a royalty of seven pence on each copy sold after allowing 200 copies for circulation the said Charles Coote, Junr. and Edward Chappell being entitled to use the melody in any separate musical composition which they may publish, free from any royalty or other consideration in respect of such use.

Charles J. Rowe

£ — 1/—

146 Holborn witness
D. G. Day. Witness

On another of the early copyright assignments of Coote and Chappell, 'Faithful ever', there appears the name of D. G. Day as a witness: at that time he was on the staff of Hopwood & Crew, but he left to become a partner in a new music publishing firm – Francis, Day & Hunter.

Today's trivia often become tomorrow's historical insights, and by good fortune some snippets of the commercial accounts from Hopwood & Crew's travellers have survived. From these we can see a typical fifteen months' business with details of journeys to various parts of the country along with the traveller's takings – these monies being from both advanced sales to dealers and actual sales to the public at the music halls. From these accounts one can see that Hopwood & Crew's business was booming and one can deduce that the trade at the New Bond Street shop must have been likewise showing a profit.

What the record market is to music publishers today, so the sheet music market was to the Victorian music publishers: as with pop record promotion today proclaiming every release 'a hit', so each music hall ballad printed at that time boasted that it was 'sung with immense success' or 'with greatest applause'.

	£	s	d
16 August 1875 Mr. Palmer's North Journey 16 August 1875 Mr. Palmer's West Journey	39	10	1
September 1875	110	16	10
October 1875	148	2	10
November 1875	96	13	1
December 1875	92	11	7
3 January 1876 Mr. Danskin's North Journey	117	5	4
23 February 1876 Mr. Palmer's North Journey	145	13	6
March 1876	126	1	5
April 1876	111	14	4
8 May 1876 Mr. Danskin's East & Midland Journey 23 May 1876 Mr. Palmer's West Journey	88	5	11
June 1876 (2 weeks' holiday)	65	16	3
5 July 1876 Mr. Danskin's North Journey	56	8	11
2 August 1876 Mr. Palmer's North Journey	94	3	10
September 1876	96	16	10
6 October 1876 Mr. Palmer's West Journey	108	19	4
13 November 1876 Mr. Palmer's North Journey			
TOTAL:	£1499	00s	1d

Hopwood & Crew Bulletin Sheet No. 1. circa 1875 which was used for general advertising in trade circles and for travellers to mark up orders.

HOPWOOD & CREW'S BULLETINS [No. 1.] Comic and Motto Songs.

ALL MUSIC HALF-PRICE AND POST FREE. MUSIC NOT IN STOCK PROCURED TO ORDER.

HOPWOOD & CREW'S

BULLETIN OF NEW MUSIC,

COMPRISING

HARRY CLIFTON'S CELEBRATED AND WORLD-RENOWNED]

Comic and Motto Songs;

HARRY CLIFTON'S CELEBRATED DRAWING-ROOM BURLESQUE DUETS,

(As sung by Miss Fanny Edwards *and* Mr. Harry Clifton, *at his popular Concerts, throughout the United Kingdom);*

The Comic Songs of the Day,

(As sung by all the leading Comic Singers, and introduced with the greatest success in all the Burlesques and Pantomimes).

HARRY CLIFTON'S CELEBRATED COMIC AND MOTTO SONGS,

As sung by him with unbounded success at his popular concerts throughout the United Kingdom.

	s.	d.
A jolly old country squire ...	3	0
As welcome as the flowers in May	3	0
A bit of my mind	3	0
An old Man's advice	3	0
Adventures of Robinson Crusoe	4	0
Agreeable young Man	3	0
Away from Demerara	3	0
Awfully jolly	3	0
A Motto for every Man ...	3	0
As long as the world goes round	3	0
A particular friend	3	0
Broken down	3	0
Bear it like a Man	3	0
Barclay's Beer	3	0
Could I live my time over again	3	0
Careless Joe	3	0
Christmas Party	3	0
Calico Printer's Clerk	3	6
Commercial Man	3	0
Charity Crow	3	0

	s.	d.
Dutchman's Courtship	3	0
Don't be after ten	3	0
Double Stout	3	0
Darby M'Guire	3	0
Elderly Beau	3	0
Farmer's Daughter of Berkshire	3	0
Fifty Years ago	3	0
Faithless Maria	3	0
Family Man	3	0
Good-tempered Man	3	0
He must have a thousand a year	3	0
Hardware Line	2	6
Have you seen the Ghost ...	3	0
Island of Green	3	0
I'll find a way or make it ...	3	0
It is better to laugh than to cry	3	0
It's not the miles we travel ...	3	0
I am one of the Olden Time ...	3	0

	s.	d.
I'm Number One	3	0
I'll go and enlist for a Sailor ...	3	0
Isabella, the Barber's Daughter	3	0
Jones's Musical Party	3	0
Jemima Brown	2	6
Look before leaping	3	0
Lannigan's Ball	3	0
Modern Times	3	0
Maria consents to be Mine ...	3	0
Musical Miseries	3	0
My old Wife and I	3	0
My rattling Mare and I ...	3	0
Mail Train Driver	2	6
Mary Ann	3	0
Merry old Uncle Joe	3	0
Michaelmas Day	3	0
My Mother-in-law	3	0
Never look behind	3	0
On Board of the Kangaroo ...	3	0

In the late 1850s, the song edition format had stabilized into an eight-page print: page 1, the cover; page 2, blank; pages 3–6, the song; page 7, a complete set of lyrics, and page 8, the back cover (usually advertising other house publications). These eight pages were formed from two folded sheets, one inside the other, allowing the pianist to remove and play from the inner sheet (pages 3–6) while the singer could retain the outer sheet wherein the lyrics were situated. By the 1890s this format was further sophisticated with the addition of the melody line and tonic solfa notation to the lyrics on page 7.

Although most songs were acquired by the publisher directly from the writer, there were cases where artistes themselves acquired works and then assigned them to the publisher – here, they forbad the use of their song to any other artiste in the music hall without their express permission, although elsewhere anyone could perform it; notices to this effect were inscribed on the front cover of the relevant music copy. As with performers today, well-known artistes could be prevailed upon (for a consideration) to perform songs which publishers sent to them – always supposing that the artiste considered these suitable for his image and style. (G. W. Hunt became the doyen of songwriters for the Lion Comiques and many other 'Minor Lions' in this way.)

London December 10th 1879.

To Messrs Hopwood & Crew.

Gentlemen

I hereby agree to sing the Song "Dont run Old England Down" during the run of the Pantomime at Covent Garden Theatre 1879. 1880. and afterwards at all My Music Hall engagements in London in consideration of your paying to me one penny royalty on each copy of said song sold, after allowing the usual copies for gratuitous distribution and trade deductions, the same as allowed by Mr H C Jewey the composer of the Song (who has also a royalty thereon) upon which I shall have no claim to royalty. And further that no other shall sing the said Song in London so long as I continue to do so. i.e. at the termination of my London engagements.

Signed

G. H. Macdermott

As there were large profits to be made from music hall songs, many back-street printers took to reproducing the foremost songs of the day without permission from the accredited publishers, and although numerous cases of song piracy were taken to court, this malpractice was never fully stamped out. The County Courts were full of aggrieved publishers suing private individuals for breach of copyright in the 1870s. In one such case, Hopwood & Crew sued George Ingram, calling such witnesses as Henri D'Alcorn and G. W. Hunt. During the evidence, Henri D'Alcorn, himself a music publisher at 351 Oxford Street, London, W, and owner of 1500 comic songs, said 'The tunes are caught up and the words are learnt from these penny books. The songs are then whistled

I George Leybourne hereby undertake to sing the song entitled "Whoa Emma" written and composed by J. J. Lonsdale at all my engagements for six months commencing from September 1st 1877 in consideration of which the said Lonsdale undertakes to pay me one half of the proceeds of the sale of the said song

Signed

20th august 1877 Geo Leybourne

about the street by every dirty urchin you meet. I have fought the question for years. I have sold between 70 000 and 90 000 copies' (of songs worth £2000 each) – 'the profit on the sale of each would be about 1s 3d or including every expense, say 1s on 18d.' G. W. Hunt gave the opinion that if he were the author of a song so pirated, he should hardly think it worthwhile to offer the copyright for sale to any publisher. He was the author of two of the pirated songs in this case – 'Don't make a noise or else you'll wake the baby' and 'Gold, Gold, Gold!' for which he was receiving royalties. When cross-examined by Ingram's lawyer, G. W. Hunt expressed his belief that the selling of pirate copies of his songs was to the detriment of the 'official' sales and therefore reduced his royalties. The verdict of the case went against the defendant, yet he was fined only 1d – such was the 'strong' deterrent to would-be copyright infringers of music hall songs!

In 1879 Henri D'Alcorn retired and auctioned all the songs in his catalogue at Brown, Swinburne and Morrell's Auction Rooms on 2 and 3 December. Auctions of part or complete catalogues were fairly common occurrences in the music trade: one can visualize the scene – most of the popular publishers would be there beforehand inspecting the music and plates, marking up the lot numbers for their attention on their brochures and then agreeing amongst themselves who would bid for what items. The firm of Hopwood & Crew acquired quite a number of copyrights in this way, and at this sale they purchased a large percentage of the D'Alcorn catalogue including copyrights from Arthur Lloyd, Vance and 'Minor Lions' such as Jolly Nash.

As one firm went into liquidation, so another was born, for it was about this time that Howard & Co was established. This firm was managed by John Matthews and Henry Ambridge – John Matthews taking full control of the

CATALOGUE

OF THE

GOODWILL AND VALUABLE STOCK

OF

Musical Copyrights

AND

Engraved Music Plates

OF

MR. J. BATH

23, BERNERS STREET,

WHO IS RETIRING FROM BUSINESS.

Which will be Sold by Auction by

MESSRS. PUTTICK & SIMPSON

AT THE SIR JOSHUA REYNOLDS GALLERIES,

47, LEICESTER SQUARE, W.C.

On Wednesday and Thursday, November 6th and 7th, 1901.

AT TEN MINUTES PAST ONE O'CLOCK PRECISELY EACH DAY.

Specimens of the Various Works may be viewed two days prior and mornings of Sale.

An example of one of the many music auctions held in the music hall era.

business when Ambridge died in 1885. His catalogue consisted purely of music hall material including songs performed by Sam Torr, Charles Chaplin, Snr, and later Marie Lloyd and George Robey. However, as Hopwood & Crew's reputation and influence as a music hall publisher grew, it overshadowed many smaller companies in this field, eventually buying them out – Howard & Co was purchased by them around the turn of the century.

The 1880s saw a period of change in the publishing business: in 1882 John Blockley died and was succeeded by his son, Thomas Blockley, who, to raise funds for the continuance of his father's business, auctioned half the catalogue on 11 to 14 June 1883. Many of the salon pieces were snapped up, yet, strangely, the music hall songs were neglected: in 1884 the first Lion Comique, George Leybourne died, heralding a divergence in tastes and styles in the music hall by artiste and audience alike: in 1886, the greatest cover illustrator, Alfred Concanen, died – his replacement was H. G. Banks, who probably knew Concanen from the days when he had worked with the printers Stannard & Dixon. He proved himself an able successor to Concanen using wit and attention to detail in much the same way as his predecessor. One of his specialities was the small insets depicting piquant scenes from the lyric and thus the music hall cover attained the semblance of an elaborate comic. This tendency was enlarged upon well into the era of the 'new' American song influences, where it was said that 'a blank was the only possible indecency in design'.

In 1888, the last of the Lion Comiques, G. H. Macdermott, ended his long friendly association with the firm of Hopwood & Crew over differences of opinion regarding the commerciality of songs which were sent to him. The

44 Oakley Road
N. Brixton. S.W.
Sept 24th '86

Dear Chas

Very well – £10 down for each song – I never sang "Where's Jenny?" at all – Don't you understand that had you taken it up – I should have withdrawn "Ochre" and substituted it! and I'm convinced in my own mind that the song would have been a "Go". The past has proved that I have been the best judge as to what would be successful – This I think you'll not dispute. From this time forth you will have no objection to my taking a song elsewhere in the event of your refusing to publish it.?

Faithfully yours
G.H. Macdermott

Chas Coote Esq

ominous undertones in Macdermott's letter to Charles Coote of 24 September 1886 leave little doubt of the rift that was opening between them.

From the mid-1880s it is noticeable that Hopwood & Crew's business policy was undergoing a change for the firm gradually moved away from the publication of purely music hall works and adapted to the new market that was opening up with the advent of musical comedy. By the 1890s the company were foremost in the musical comedy field publishing 'The Geisha' and the first American success of this genre 'The Belle of New York'. At the death of Edward Chappell, Charles Coote became sole managing director and the company became limited in 1898.

On 26 April 1904, Thomas Blockley died intestate, and his son, Thomas Trotter Blockley, sold up his business interests and catalogue to the music publishing and piano making company of E. Ascherberg & Co. In 1906, at the end of the British music hall era, the two firms of Hopwood & Crew Ltd and E. Ascherberg & Co merged to form Ascherberg, Hopwood & Crew Ltd with Eugene Ascherberg as its sole managing director. Although Charles Coote was no longer actively involved in the new company, he maintained an interest in the firm, now at 16 Mortimer Street. A pamphlet celebrating the merger states: '. . . but the portly form of Charles Coote, the jovial countenance, thick white hair and heavy gold eye-glasses were a familiar sight to all at Mortimer Street, where he was a constant visitor.'

In 1969 Ascherberg, Hopwood & Crew Ltd was taken over by Chappell & Co Ltd – thus completing the circle in a relationship which began with Edward Chappell. The priceless heritage of the music hall has been handed down to us today in the form of sheet music stock, letters and contracts dating

I, Henry Bellamy landlord of the premises in No. 5 St. Maur Road Fulham Road

do hereby acknowledge that the Piano now standing and being on the premises above mentioned is the property of Messrs. E. Ascherberg & Co., of 46, Berners Street, London, W., and not of the tenant of the said premises. And I hereby agree with Messrs. E. Ascherberg & Co., at their request, not to distrain upon the said Piano for any rent or other moneys which may be or may hereafter become due from the tenant of the said premises for the term of three years from the date hereof.

Dated this 12th day of November 1896

Witness Beatrice Bellamy

Henry Bellamy

A licence for the issue of E. Ascherberg piano – the Victorian equivalent of a juke box licence today.

from those times: in this book a *small* amount of this heritage has been compiled, reproducing as faithfully as possible the history and colourful atmosphere of the halls. In order to make this book less cumbersome, however, the songs reproduced herein have been slightly reduced in dimensions (the original copies measuring up to $10\frac{1}{2}$ inches by 14 inches), and because of the need to include more examples of our music hall heritage, pages 2 and 8 from the eight page songs – those originally being blank or set aside for advertisements – have been omitted.

As you turn over the following pages, you will also be turning back the pages of social history, encountering the artistes – the stars of their day – and discovering anew the wit and tunefulness of the songs that they sang: but first, in true music hall style, we present our programme . . .

3. Programme

1. Bacon & Greens .... *Sam Cowell & Arthur Lloyd*
2. Hop Light Loo .... *T. Mackney*
3. Polly Perkins of Paddington Green.......... *Harry Clifton*
4. Ticket of Leave Man .... *Alfred Vance*
5. Slap Bang, Here We Are Again.............. *Alfred Vance*
6. Up in a Balloon .... *George Leybourne*
7. Fashionable Fred .... *Walter Laburnum*
8. Brown the Tragedian .... *Arthur Lloyd*
9. The Rustic Damsel........................ *Harry Liston*
10. Captain Cuff .... *George Leybourne*
11. Dear Old Pals .... *G. H. Macdermott*
12. Little Miss Muffet sat on a Tuffet .... *G. H. Macdermott*
13. Tuner's Oppor-Tuner-Ty .... *Fred Coyne*
14. The Bulls Won't Bellow.................... *Sam Torr*
15. In my fust 'Usband's Time .... *Herbert Campbell*
16. Up went the Price........................ *G. H. Macdermott*
17. Baa Baa Baa .... *Jolly Nash*
18. She does the Fandango all over the Place ...... *Henri Clark*
19. The House that Jerry built .... *James Fawn*
20. What Cheer Ria .... *Bessie Bellwood*
21. The Boy in the Gallery .... *Nelly Power*
22. The Funny Things They Do upon the Sly ..... *G. W. Hunter*
23. Angels without Wings .... *Vesta Tilley*
24. Ti! Hi! Tiddelly Hi! .... *Harry Rickards*
25. Buy me some Almond Rock .... *Marie Lloyd*
26. Oh! Mr Porter............................ *Marie Lloyd*
27. So her Sister says .... *Jenny Valmore*
28. Catch 'Em Alive Oh! .... *Gus Elen*
29. That Gorgonzola Cheese .... *Harry Champion*
30. Slight Mistake on the Part of my Valet .... *George Robey*
31. The Bobbies of the Queen .... *Maud Santley*
32. On the day King Edward gets his Crown on .... *Harry Pleon*
33. An Old Man's Darling .... *Vesta Victoria*

INTERVAL

ENCORE

34. Beautiful Dora............................ *George Leybourne/G. H. Macdermott*
35. She's so Sweet (Sweet, Sweet, Sweet) .... *G. H. Macdermott*

Mr SAM: COWELL

WITH IMMENSE APPLAUSE

AT HIS POPULAR CONCERTS THROUGHOUT

ENGLAND, IRELAND, & SCOTLAND

UNDER THE MANAGEMENT OF

Mr MORISON KYLE

ENT. STA. HALL. PRECE 6D

GLASGOW

MORISON KYLE. MUSIC REPOSITORY

108 QUEEN STREET

OPPOSITE ROYAL EXCHANGE

WHERE MAY BE HAD Mr SAM COWELLS FAVORITE SONGS.

"VILLIAM VILLIAMS REVENGE" "BETSY KNUBBLES OR THE MAID OF ALL WORK" "CLEAN YOUR BOOTS" "ARTFULL DODGER" &C. &C.

BACON AND GREENS.

What a thrill of re_mem_brance e'en now they a wa_ken, Of child_hood's gay morning, and youths mer_ry scenes, When one day, we had greens and a plate full of ba_con, And the next we had ba_con and a plate full of greens..
When the Banks re_fused spe_cie and cre_dit was sha_ken I shared in the wreck and was ruin_ed in means, My friends all de_cla_red I had not saved my ba_con, But I liv_ed for I still had my ba_con and greens..
Oh there is a charm in this dish right_ly ta_ken That from cus_tards and jel_lies an Epi_cure weans Stick your fork in the fat wrap your greens round the ba_con, And you'll vow their is no dish like good ba_con and greens..
1st. SYM.
GO TO *
2nd. SYM.
GO TO *
3rd. SYM.
GO TO 𝄋
V. S.

sf.
I re _ turn to con_fess that for once I'm mis _ ta_ken, As
much as I've known of lif's chan _ geable scenes, There's one dish that's e _ qual to
both greens and bacon And that is a dish of good ba _ con and greens

HOP LIGHT LOO,

PRINTED BY L'ENFANT

SUNG WITH GREAT SUCCESS BY

MACKNEY,

WRITTEN EXPRESSLY FOR HIM BY

G. WARE,

ENT, STA. HALL,

Pr. 2/6

LONDON: HOPWOOD & CREW, 42, NEW BOND STREET, W.

HOP LIGHT LOO!

WRITTEN BY GEORGE WARE

ARRANGED BY GEORGE BICKNELL.

used to meet my charmer when I'd nothing else to do And I'm
sure I ne'er will harm her My lovely darling Loo.
CHORUS.
Then hop light Loo and
shew your pretty feet, You are a charming creature I always like to meet. Then
hop light Loo, and do the best you can, And when you want a part_ner

I'm the ve--ry man.
Oh, I'm a handsome nigger as
ev_er you did see, Teeth as white as i_vo_ry, and skin like e_bo_ny. My
hair is crisp and curly My heart is firm and true But I think I'll throw myself away and

CHORUS.
marry lovely Loo. Then hop light Loo, and shew your pretty feet, You
are a charming creature I always like to meet. Then hop light Loo and
do the best you can And when you want a part_ner I'm the very man.

3

I took her to a ball one night the darkies all did stare,
To see my pretty nigger gal the fairest of the fair.
She trip't on the fantastic as light as fairies do,
Star of the night in colors bright was my lovely Loo.
Then hop light Loo, &c.

4

Now your shoes they shall be satin, your stockings shall be silk.
Your dress it shall be muslin as white as any milk.
We'll ride off to the parson's, donkies we'll have two.
One shall be for me to ride, and the other lovely Loo.
Then hop light Loo, &c.

5

I'll marry her tomorrow and take her right away,
She never shall see sorrow but bless the happy day.
I'll buy my love a bonnet and a hoop-de-dooden-doo,
And I'll write a marriage sonnet on my lovely darling Loo.
Then hop light Loo, &c.

POLLY PERKINS OF PADDINGTON GREEN

OR THE

BROKEN HEARTED MILKMAN.

She was beautiful as a Butterfly. As proud as a Queen,
Was pretty little Polly Perkins Of Paddington Green

WRITTEN & SUNG, WITH TUMULTUOUS APPLAUSE, BY

HARRY CLIFTON.

LONDON HOPWOOD & CREW L^TD 42 NEW BOND STREET, W.

POLLY PERKINS OF PADDINGTON GREEN.

Written and Composed by
HARRY CLIFTON.

Arranged by
J. CANDY.

N. B. *This Song is legally protected, and cannot be sung in Public without the written permission of the Author.*

keep - - ing of the com - pa - ny of a young ser - - vant
maid; Who liv - èd on board wa - - - ges, the
house to keep clean, In a gen - - - tle - - - man's
fam' - ly near Pad - ding - ton Green.
To be sung ad lib:
Oh! she was as

CHORUS.
Beau-ti--ful as a But-ter-fly, and as proud as a
Queen, Was pret-ty lit-tle Pol--ly Per--kins of
Pad-ding-ton Green.
f

2. Her eyes were as black as the pips of a pear, No
3. When I'd rat - tle in a morn - ing, and cry "milk be - - - - low" At the
rose in the gar - den with her cheeks could com - pare, Her
sound of my milk cans her face she would show, With a
hair hung in 'ringerlets' so beau - ti - ful and long. I
smile up - - on her countenance and a laugh in her eye, If I
thought that she lov'd me, but found I was wrong. Oh! she was as
thought she'd have lov'd me, I'd have laid down to die, For she was as
ad lib:

4.
When I ask-ed her to marry me, she said, "Oh what stuff" And told me to
"drop it for she'd had quite enough Of my nonsense" At the same time I'd been ve-ry kind, But to
mar-ry a milk man she didn't feel in-clin'd. Oh she was as
CHOS & SYM: as before.
5.
"Oh the man that has me must have sil--ver and gold, A cha-riot to
ride in, and be hand-some and bold; His hair must be cur--ly as a---ny watch-
spring, And his whiskers as big as a brush for clothing." Oh she was as
CHOS & SYM: as before.
6.
The words that she ut-ter'd went straight thro' my heart, I sob---bed, I
sigh-ed, and straight did de-part With a tear on my eye-lid as big as a
bean, Bidding good-bye to Polly and Paddington Green. Ah she was as
CHOS & SYM: as before.
7.
In six months she married this hard-heart-ed girl, But it was not a
'Wi-count', and it was not a 'Nearl', It 'was not a 'Bar-ro-nite' but a shade or two
'wus' 'Twas a bow legg'd Con-duc-tor of a Twopenny 'Bus. In spite of all she was as
CHOS & SYM:

H & C. 1382.

TICKET OF LEAVE MAN.

WRITTEN & SUNG

BY

VANCE.

AT THE

STRAND, PAVILION, & METROPOLITAN MUSIC HALLS,

WITH DEAFNING ACCLAMATIONS.

ENT. STA. HALL.

LONDON; HOPWOOD & CREW, 42, NEW BOND STREET, W.

Pr. 2/6

THE TICKET OF LEAVE MAN.

Written and Sung by A. G. VANCE. Music by M. HOBSON.

*(tenner) ten years.

Sir Georgey Grey, Wot granted a ticket - of - leaf.
2nd Verse.
I got home here in time for to see Wor--
mald and Marsden fight,
Lots of vatches vent that day Vich a-
ff
mp
ff
mp
rit.

*("stooks!") pocket handkerchief.

3.

There's a "ticket-of-leaf man" now I'd pick,
A proper example to all young "guns"*
I means the wun at the 'Ryal 'Lympic,
Who increas'd the treasurer's "funs"
But he ain't like me for I like to thieve,
Though the "perlice" is werry 'ot,
I'm good to "dip" or "crack a crib;"
But I spurns the "wile garotte."
Who I is, &c.

4.

The Brothers' Davenport's little game
To nothink seems to dwindle,
Since Professor Handerson did show
Like his Magic 'twas a swindle.
Now there's a knot I'd like to see
The Davenports' untie it,
I means the one wot Calcraft does,
They isn't game to try it.
Who I is, &c.

5.

Now there's swindles great as well as small
But of swindles whatsomdever,
That wun in the vine-trade lately done
By a "Witt_y man not clever,
A Hog's-head sich as his desarves
A Punching and be throttled,
He took a drop too much of the draught,
So by Government he's bottled
Who I is, &c.

6

Oh there's a dodge wot did come out,
Of swindles a colossus,
A mechanical 'ead wot sings, 'tis said
Called a Hanthropoglossos.
By electric means it sings, its song,
But the public they did book it
With the "Rogue's March" from St James's Hall
Vith a shock electric hooked it.
So now adoo each worthy pal,
My wisit must be brief,
But return and see you again I shall
When I'll bring my "ticket-of-leaf."

H. DAVISON, LITHO. 22, BROOKS MEWS, NEW BOND ST

(*"*young guns*") pickpockets.

H & C. 688.

150TH EDITION.

NOTICE *The Public are cautioned against Spurious Copies of this Song the Original Edition being Published solely by* H. D'ALCORN.

AS SUNG BY FRANK HALL.
ALSO
VANCE & T MACLAGAN.

JOLLY DOGS
WE'RE ALL JOLLY DOGS
SUCH JOLLY DOGS ARE WE
OR
SLAP BANG
HERE WE ARE AGAIN.

Ent. Sta. Hall. Price 3/-

LONDON
H. D'ALCORN, BLENHEIM HOUSE, 351, OXFORD ST. W.

SLAP BANG, HERE WE ARE AGAIN. OR

THE SCHOOL OF JOLLY DOGS.

WRITTEN BY

HARRY COPELAND.

Just Published. The Ladies version of this popular song, "WE ARE ALL JOLLY GIRLS." pr: 2/6

✳ *From this sign to ⌖ p:3. may be omitted at pleasure.*

dance, they sing, they laugh ha, ha, they
laugh ha, ha, they dance, they sing, what
jol ----- ly dogs are we, Fal la la, fal la la,
fal la la, fal la la, fal la la, fal la la,

Fal de the ral, de the ral lal li do, Slap, bang,
here we are a-gain, here we are a-gain, here we are a-gain,
Slap, bang, here we are a-gain, What jol-ly dogs are
we.
ff

2

They meet each night at six o'clock,
And then sit down to dine;
They put the courses out of sight,
And then they take their wine,
And they always seem so jolly oh!
So jolly oh! so jolly oh!

3

At eight o'clock they sally forth,
Because you know its dark;
"Follow my leader" cries the chief,
To night we'll have a lark;
And they always seem so jolly oh!
So jolly oh! so jolly oh!

4

To balls or hops of course they go,
And each man does his weed;
They stick by one another
As they're previously agreed,
And they always seem so jolly oh!
So jolly oh! so jolly oh!

5

Spring-heel Jack and all his pals
With their nocturnal larks,
I'm sure were not a patch upon
This school of modern sparks;
For they always seem so jolly oh!
So jolly oh! so jolly oh!

This popular Melody may also be had, Arranged as a MARCH by the great VANCE. pr. 2/6

UP IN A BALLOON,

Up in a balloon, up in a balloon,
All amongst the little stars, and round about the moon.
Up in a balloon, up in a balloon,
It's something awful jolly to be up in a balloon

SUNG WITH IMMENSE SUCCESS BY

GEORGE LEYBOURNE.

WRITTEN & COMPOSED BY

G. W. HUNT.

London: HOPWOOD & CREW: 42, New Bond St. W.

PRICE 3/-

UP IN A BALLOON.

Written and Composed by G. W. HUNT.

H & C. 1456.

One night I went up in a bal_loon, On a
f
voyage of dis_covery to vi_sit the moon, Where an old man dwells, so some
peo_ple say_"Thro' cut_ting of sticks on a Sun_____day." Up
went the bal_loon quick_ly high_er and high_er, O_ver

house-top and chimney-pot, tow-er and spire, I knock'd off the Monument's
top ve-ry nigh, And caught hold of the cross of St. Paul's go-ing by.
CHORUS.
Up in a bal----loon..... Up in a bal--loon.....
ff
All among the lit--tle stars sail--ing round the moon....

Up in a bal_ _ _ _ _ loon . . . . Up in a bal_

loon . . . . It's some_thing aw_ _ _ _ful jol_ _ly to be

Up in a bal_ _ _ _ _loon . . . . . .

f

8va

"UP IN A BALLOON."

WRITTEN AND COMPOSED BY G. W. HUNT.

1

One night I went up in a balloon,
On a voyage of discovery to visit the moon,
Where an old man lives, so some people say—
"Through cutting of sticks on a Sunday."
Up went the balloon quickly higher and higher,
Over house-top and chimney-pot, tower and spire,
I knocked off the Monument's top very nigh,
And caught hold of the Cross of Saint Pauls going by.

CHORUS.
Up in a balloon, up in a balloon,
All among the little stars sailing round the moon,
Up in a balloon, up in a balloon,
It's something awful jolly to be up in a balloon.

2

Up, up I was borne with terrible power,
At the rate of ten thousand five hundred an hour,
The air was cold, the wind blew loud,
I narrowly escaped being choked by a cloud;
Still up I went till surrounded by stars,
And such Planets as Jupiter, Venus and Mars,
The Big and the Little Bear, loudly did growl,
And the Dog Star on seeing me set up a howl!
Whilst, Up in a balloon, up in a balloon, &c.

3

I met shooting stars who were bent upon sport,
But who "shot" in a very strange manner I thought,
And one thing beat all by chalks I must say,
That was when I got into the Milky Way;
I counted the stars, till at last I thought,
I'd found out how much they were worth by the quart,
An unpolite "Aerolite" who ran 'gainst my ear,
Wouldn't give "*e'er a light*," to light my cigar.
Whilst, Up in a balloon, up in a balloon &c.

4

Next a comet went by 'midst fire like hail,
To give me a lift, I seized hold of his tail,
To where he was going I didn't enquire,
We'd gone past the moon, till we couldn't get higher;
Yes we'd got to the furthermost!! don't think I joke
When somehow I felt a great shock— I awoke!
When instead of balloon, moon and planets, I saw,
I'd tumbled from off of my bed to the floor.

CHORUS.
And there was no balloon,— there was no balloon,
There were not any planets, and there wasn't any moon,
So never sup too heavy or by jingo very soon,
You're like to fancy you are going up in a balloon.

FASHIONABLE FRED,

"Yes I'm just about the cut for Belgravia,
To keep the proper pace I know the plan,
Wire in and go a head then for Fashionable Fred,
I'm Fashionable Fred the ladies' man"

SUNG WITH DISTINGUISHED SUCCESS BY

WALTER LABURNUM,

WRITTEN BY **WALTER BURNOT,** MUSIC BY **J. CONWAY BROWN.**

ENT. STA. HALL.

London; HOPWOOD & CREW, 42, New Bond St. W.
OFFICE OF "BOND STREET" MUSICAL MONTHLY MAGAZINE,
NEW & POPULAR SONGS, BALLADS, & DANCE MUSIC, PRICE ONE SHILLING.

PRICE 3/-

FASHIONABLE FRED.

Written by WALTER BURNOT.

Composed by J. CONWAY BROWN.

look'd on as the cheese, and all the girls I please, I'm a model swell of e_legance and
grace......... Wire in and go a-head, then, for Fashiona_ble Fred, Pit
pat's the way, and sharp a_bout the word........ Give me suf_ficient cash, then
see me cut a dash, For what_e_ver's slow in my i_dea's ab_ _surd..........
Ped:
Ped:

CHORUS.

Yes I'm just a_bout the cut for Bel_ _ _ _ gra_ _ _ _ _ _ _ _ _ _ _via To
f
keep the proper pace I know the plan...... Wire in and go a_head then for
Fa_shiona_ble Fred I'm Fashion_a_ble Fred the la_dies' man.....
Ped:
f

2. My life from first to last, has been jol--ly, gay and fast, In
3. This is the age for dash, and all must come out flash, If
4. Tho' in the Park I walk, and with the la--dies talk, My
f
fact to find a fast--er you'd be teas'd.... In ev'-rything I'm quick, the
in this world they try to make their way...... If you wear a seed-y dress, you'll
tai--lors bills I al--ways like to run....... I can-ter in the Row and
yan-kee's call it stick, I'm some-thing like a flash of lightning
find to your dis-tress, All your friends will quick-ly turn their heads a-
when to balls I go, I ga----lop with the charming girls like

 H.DAVISON, LITHO. 22, BROOKS MEWS NEW BOND ST

BROWN THE TRAGEDIAN
(NO MATTER!)

WRITTEN BY **G. W. HUNT,**

SUNG BY **ARTHUR LLOYD.**

LONDON,
H. D'ALCORN & Co
(BLENHEIM HOUSE.)
351, OXFORD STREET, W.
L'ENFANT & WHITE, IMPT

Price 3/-

JUNIUS BROWN THE TRAGEDIAN.

("NO MATTER.")

SUNG BY
ARTHUR LLOYD.

WRITTEN & COMPOSED
BY
C. W. HUNT.

I'm an ac---tor who's seen bet---ter days, ... For I
p
once was a star I've a no---tion; I've been
toss'd a------bout all sorts of ways, ... Up---
--on the the-------a------tri-------cal o---cean; But

jea-lou-sy, spite and all that, ... Has brought

me down to but a seed-y 'un; It's been

all caus'd thro' en-vy, that's flat, ... For I

once was a hea-vy tra-ge-di-an.

CHORUS.
I've been a bright star in my time . . . . . Tho'
now I'm reduced to a seedy 'un, In me you may please to be--
-----hold . . . . Ju----ni---------us Brown the tra---ge---di----an.
repeat f.
f

JUNIUS BROWN THE TRAGEDIAN. OR "NO MATTER."

I'm an actor who's seen better days,
For I once was a star I've a notion;
I've been toss'd about all sorts of ways
Upon the theatrical ocean.
But jealousy, spite and all that
Has brought me down to but a seedy 'un
It's been all caus'd by envy, - that's flat,
For I once was a heavy tragedian.

CHORUS. I've been a bright star in my time,
Though now I'm reduced to a seedy 'un;
In me you may please to behold -
Junius Brown the Tragedian.

You have all seen my name in the bills,
Which is Junius Antonius Brown, sirs;
And I flatter myself I have caused -
Great excitement in many a town, sirs;
My last 'shop' was the Garrick, Whitechapel;
In a 'part' that I could above any fit,
My 'screw' sirs, for only six nights
Was two pounds and half a clear benefit.

SPOKEN. - That was money, but what do they offer talent now? I was actually offered the other day twenty-five 'bob' per week to play Othello, the Clown in the Pantomime, and do bill-sticking in the morning. Did I accept it? Blood and blue fire! Never! NEVER! but no matter, a time may come when they will be glad to secure the services of Brown the Tragedian. CHORUS.

Since Kemble none like me's been seen,
Yet nought but bad luck is my portion;
My friends say I'm better than Kean,
That my Richard' and 'Hamlet's' a caution.
They say my declaiming's a treat -
In the speech over Cæsar by Antony;
I can do the soft parts low and sweet,
Likewise I can 'pile up the agony.'

SPOKEN. - For two consecutive weeks was I the leading attraction at the Royal Bower, and should have startled the world at Drury Lane; but for professional malice. I am kept off the boards out of fear. They know I should render Shakespeare's great characters as they have never been rendered before. My reading of his plays is entirely different to Macready, Kean, Phelps, T. C. King and all those fellows, - They know that. - but no matter, a time may come when they will cringe to Brown the Tragedian. CHORUS.

I search through the 'Era' each week
And I 'write in' when talent's required,
But they say they don't know me. (there's cheek
Of such insults and envy I'm tired.)
They offer me terms for a 'super,'
Or ask if I'm up to 'utility.'
But I'll starve and remain as I am -
An artiste of wondrous ability.

SPOKEN. - Me, ME! Junius Antonius Brown descend to do the cock in Hamlet, or Bobby in the Pantomime. Ye Gods and small fishes! Rather would I descend from my pedestal of fame and become a comic vocalist. but no matter! NO MATTER!! The time may come when they will be glad to pile gold at the feet of Brown the Tragedian.

CHORUS.

THE RUSTIC DAMSEL

MR H. LISTON, FROM A PHOTOGRAPH BY M. ALLEN & C^O DUBLIN.

SUNG BY

HARRY LISTON,

IN HIS POPULAR ENTERTAINMENT "MERRY MOMENTS."

AUTHOR OF

FANCY GOES A VERY LONG WAY	4	GRANDFATHER SHOREHAM	4
HES WORSE THAN MY BIG BROTHER	4	MERRY MOMENTS	4
DID YOU KNOW MR SMIT	4	ANY VINDER'S TO MEND	4

LONDON: JOHN BLOCKLEY, 3, ARGYLL ST REGENT ST W.

"THE RUSTIC YOUNG DAMSEL."

Also in the key of B♭.

Words by
T. DODSWORTH.

Arranged by.
J. HOLBROOK.

A long time a _ _ go, I re _ _ mem _ ber it well, In a
p
beau _ ti _ ful vil _ lage a dam _ sel did dwell; A _ _
lone with her pa _ rents she lived all se _ _ rene, Her
age it was red, and her hair was nine _ _ teen.
SPOKEN
THE RUSTIC YOUNG DAMSEL. IN C.
HOLBROOK.

Published by John Blockley 3 Argyll St. Regent St. W.

THE RUSTIC YOUNG DAMSEL.

A long time ago, I remember it well,
In a beautiful village a damsel did dwell;
Alone with her parents she lived all serene,
Her age it was red, and her hair was nineteen.

Spoken: Yes she was a generous girl, she supported plain needlework by taking in her poor old father. She was called *Chorus.*—

A sweet rustic damsel with cheeks like the rose,
A roman shaped eye, and a cast in her nose.

Now she had a lovier who close by did dwell,
A bandy backed rustic and hump legged as well;
Said he, "Fly with me by the light of yon star,
For you are the eye of my apple you are."

Spoken: He was poor, but he was honest, and many an honest coat beats beneath a ragged heart, and he loved

Chorus.— A sweet rustic damsel &c.

But this dutiful maiden said gently, "Be wise;
My father would scratch out my nails with his eyes.
If you love me you will not bring me to disgrace,"
Sobbed the maid as she buried her hands in her face.

Spoken: It was an affecting scene and the light of a cloud suddenly bursting from behind the moon fully revealed the attitude of

Chorus.— A sweet rustic damsel &c.

So as she refused him he knocked down the maid,
Then silently opened the knife of his blade
He next cut the throat of this damsel so fair,
Then dragged her along by the head of her hair.

Spoken: It was all her own hair; she never descended to false chignons but she was dead now. Yes her throat was cut from mouth to mouth and the water rushed forth from the wound like blood

Chorus.— A sweet rustic damsel &c.

Just then her old father came up it appears
And look'd on this sad sight with eyes in his tears
He knelt by her side and her sweet face he kiss'd;
Then rushed with his nose at the murderer's fist.

Spoken: Poor old man! He had put his head on his hat and come out in search of his absent daughter and had just stopped to strike his pipe against a match, when he saw the dead body of

Chorus.— A sweet rustic damsel &c.

With the knife the old man he an end to him put;
Then spurned with his body the murderer's foot;
To commit suicide then his way he did wend,
So that is the tale of a very sad end.

Spoken: Poor old man! His was the fate to be lamented, cut off in the flower of his youth. In the bloom of womanhood she died. Her memory was short but her life is still revered by those who knew

Chorus.— A sweet rustic damsel &c.

LEYBOURNE'S

CAPTAIN CUFF.

COMIC SONG

WRITTEN & COMPOSED BY

G. W. HUNT.

SUNG WITH IMMENSE SUCCESS BY

GEORGE LEYBOURNE.

Pr. 4/-

LONDON; HOPWOOD & CREW, 42, NEW BOND STREET. W.

LEYBOURNE'S

CAPTAIN CUFF.

Written and Composed by G. W. HUNT.

Some coons go in for whis - kers, some For
mf
most un - - plea - - sant Dogs, Some
fel - - lows have a weak - - ness for The
most out - - ra - - geous Togs, I'm

ve - - ry strong on lin - - en Yes And
would - - not give a dol - - lar For
life with - - out a splen - - did show Of
snow white cuff and col - - lar!

CHORUS.
Captain Cuff; Captain Cuff. You can tell me by my collar, Captain Cuff, Captain
ff
Cuff tho I'm not worth half a dol_lar I'm aw'fly stiff in style as my
ci_garette I puff They cry "Hi!" clear the way here comes Captain Cuff.
f
Cres.

1

Some coons go in for whiskers, some
For most unpleasant Dogs,
Some fellows have a weakness for
The most outrageous "Togs."
I'm very strong on linen, yes,
And wouldn't give a dollar—
For life, without a splendid show,
Of snow white cuff and collar.

(SPOKEN) Which has earned for me the title of—

Captain Cuff, Captain Cuff, you can tell me by my collar,
Captain Cuff, Captain Cuff, tho' I'm not worth half a dollar,
I'm awfully stiff in style, as my cigarette I puff,
They cry "Hi! clear the way here comes Captain Cuff."

2

Sometimes a common fellow,
Of the "lower order" class,
Will dare to make some rude remark,
Or mock me as I pass;
And lots of vulgar little boys,
They know me well enough,
And oft salute me in the street,
With—"What cheer Capting Cuff."

"Capting Cuff, Capting Cuff you can tell him by his collar,
"Capting Cuff, Capting Cuff he ain't worth half a dollar,
"He's "Glenfield" in his style, as his cigarette he'll puff,
"So hi! hey! clear the way, here comes Capting Cuff."

4

I lounge about at parties,
I'm "heavy" at the Ball,
By Jove! "the Captain" never has
To decorate a wall;
I dance with every charmer fit,
To be my vis-a-vis,
And 'tis awfully delightful,
How the ladies follow me.

(SPOKEN.) With their eyes all over the room, when I often hear a charming creature observe to her Ma—"O Ma dear, who is that handsome, dignified party ovar there?" then by the time I've struck an imposing attitude I hear the "old un" say "Why my *dear* Maud don't you know It's—(*Chos.*) Captain Cuff, you can tell him, &c.

5

With darling eyes upon me,
Thro' life I'll gaily march,
My style shall be the stiffest,
My motto shall be "Starch."
Should my cuff and collar glory
Be ever gone and fled,
You'll know that Captain Cuff's gone wrong,
Or his washerwomans dead!

(SPOKEN) And what is all the world to a man when his Laundress is defunct, it would mean ruin to—(*Chos.*) Captain Cuff, &c.

DEAR OLD PALS.

Dear old pals, jolly old pals!
Clinging together in all sorts of weather,
Dear old pals, jolly old pals,
Give me the friendship of dear old pals.

WRITTEN & COMPOSED BY

G. W. HUNT,

SUNG WITH IMMENSE SUCCESS BY

G. H. MACDERMOTT.

ENT STA HALL

Pr 2/- net.

London: ASCHERBERG, HOPWOOD & CREW, Ltd., 16, Mortimer Street, W.

PRINTED IN ENGLAND.

DEAR OLD PALS.

Written and Composed by G. W. HUNT.

H & C. 1878.

I like my share of plea - - sure, and I'll
have it while I can, I
love a lov - - ing wo - - man, and Res -
- pect an hon - - est man; I

like to find true friend - ship in The
life that's roll - - ing by, And
such is al - - ways found be - - tween, My
old Pal Tom and I.

CHORUS. TEMPO DI VALSE.

Lowe & Brydone Ltd. Printers London, N.W. 10.

1

I like my share of pleasure, and
I'll have it while I can,
I love a loving woman, and
Respect an honest man;
I like to find true friendship in
The life that's rolling by,
And such is always found between
My old pal Tom and I.

CHORUS.

We're dear old pals, jolly old pals!
Clinging together in all sorts of weather,
Dear old pals, jolly old pals,
Give me the friendship of dear old pals!

2

We've tasted of the "Ups" of life,
We've also felt its "Downs,"
Sometimes our pockets held bright gold,
And sometimes only "browns"
And be our drink bright sparkling "Cham,"
Or merely humble beer,
The grasp of friendship's been the same,
Through each succeeding year.

Chorus. Like dear old pals, &c.

3

We do snug little dinners, and
They pass off very nice,
I put my old pal in the chair,
He makes me take the vice;
We toast her Gracious Majesty,
We don't forget "the gals,"
But *the* toast of the evening is
"Success to true old pals!"

CHORUS.

We're dear old pals, jolly old pals,
Clinging together in all sorts of weather,
Dear old pals, jolly old pals,
Give me the friendship of dear old pals!

4

It's ever been my maxim, yes,
And so it ever shall,
To help a stranger when I can,
But never desert a pal!
And after winning life's hard fight,
What sweet reward is found,
In a conscience clear, a heart that's light
And dear old pals around!

Chorus. Still dear old pals, &c.

H & C. 1878.

LITTLE MISS MUFFET SAT ON A TUFFET.

PRINTED & PUBD
AS THE ACT DIRECTS
[illegible] 22ND 18[illegible]

WORDS BY
JOSEPH S. LONG.

MUSIC BY
ERNEST J. SYMONS.

SUNG WITH IMMENSE SUCCESS BY
G. H. MACDERMOTT.

LONDON: HOPWOOD & CREW. 42. NEW BOND ST. W.

Pr 4/.

"LITTLE MISS MUFFET."

Written by
JOSEPH S. LONG.

Composed by
ERNEST J. SYMONS.

Miss Muf_fet once went for a walk in the Park, With
Si_mon a sim_ple young lad.................. And
did not re_turn to her home un_til dark, Then
seemed to be aw_ful_ly sad.................. Why

what is the mat _ ter? the Ma' she ex _ claim'd Miss
Muf _ fet then sniv _ ell'd and sighed .... And
Si _ mon he trem _ bled and seem'd quite a _ shamed At
length with a sigh he re _ _ plied ....

CHORUS.
Lit_tle Miss Muffet sat on a tuf_fet, Eat_ing her curds and
whey,...... When a lit_tle big spider, Sat close down be_side her, And,
that's all I've got to say................. say.........
1st time.
2nd time.
f

1

Miss Muffet once went for a walk in the Park,
With Simon a simple young lad,
And did not return to her home until dark,
Then seemed to be awfully sad.
"Why what is the matter?" the Ma she exclaimed,
Miss Muffet then snivell'd, and sighed,
And Simon he trembled and seemed quite ashamed,
At length, with a sigh, he replied: -

CHORUS.

Little Miss Muffet sat on a tuffet,
Eating her Curds and Whey,
When a little "Big" spider
Sat close down beside her,
And, that's all I've got to say.

2

What ailed this young lady, the Ma' could not tell,
At length she called in Doctor Quack,
Who said she'd be worse much, before she got well,
He called it a bilious attack;
At last she confessed to her mother, and said
Young Simon had called her a "Pet;"
And made her a promise that they should be wed,
Yet all they from Simon could get:
Chorus. Little Miss Muffet &c.

3

The father remarked that a spider he knew,
Advantage will take of a fly;
But tho' many wonderful things they can do,
They cannot cause maidens to sigh.
So he, for a promise of marriage, a breach,
Of Simon, did damages claim;
The lawyer for her, made a capital speech,
Then, Simon did boldly exclaim.

CHORUS.

Little Miss Muffet sat on a tuffet,
Eating her Curds and Whey,
When a little "Big" spider
Sat close down beside her,
And, that's all I've got to say.

4

The case was so strange that Magistrate said,
"You'd better both make yourselves one,"
They took his advice, and anon they were wed,
And Simon was blessed with a son.
They quarrelled, so Simon one day with the boy,
To some distant country did flee,
Now daily he sits all alone in his joy
And sings with the child on his knee.
Chorus. Little Miss Muffet &c.

Berridge, Bros. Engravers & Steam Lithos.

TUNER'S OPPOR-TUNER-TY.

WORDS BY

HARRY ADAMS.

COMPOSED & SUNG BY

FRED COYNE.

ENT. STA. HALL

Pr. 3/-

LONDON: HOWARD & Co 28, Gt MARLBOROUGH St W

STANNARD & SON.

THE TUNER'S OPPOR-TUN-ITY.

COMPOSED BY FRED. COYNE. ARRANGED BY WILLIAM SIM.

Miss Crot_chet_y Qua_ver was sweet se_ven_teen, And a
p
play_er of ex_cel_lent skill,
She would
play all the day, all the ev_'ning as well, Mak_ing
all the neigh_bour_hood ill
And to

keep her pi - an - o in tune she would have, A
good tu - ner con - stant - ly there, And he'd
pull up the in - stru - ment three times a week, Just to
keep it in pro - per re - pair.
ad lib

CHORUS.
And first he'd tune it gen_tly, then he'd tune it strong, Then he'd touch a
mf
2nd time ff and play in octaves.
short note, then he'd run a _ long, Then he'd go with ven_geance, e _
nough to break the key, At last he tuned when e'er he got an op_por_tu_ni _
_ ty.
tempo 1o
f

1

Miss Crotchety Quaver was sweet seventeen,
And a player of excellent skill,
She would play all the day, all the ev'ning as well,
Making all the neighbourhood ill.
And to keep her Piano in tune she would have
A good tuner constantly there,
And he'd pull up the instrument three times a week,
Just to keep it in proper repair.
And first he'd tune it gently, then he'd tune it strong,
Then he'd touch a short note, then he'd run along,
Then he'd go with vengeance enough to break the key,
At last he tuned whene'er he got an oppor-tuner-ty.

2

He came there so often I thought I'd complain,
That in March, April, May, and in June,
That tuner had been there once ev'ry day,
To keep her Piano in tune.
I said, "He's too often here hang-ing about,
And he's costing you no end of pelf,
If your instrument wants such a lot of repairs,
I'll attend to the business myself."

CHORUS.

3

But vainly I spoke to Miss Crotchety Q.—
She said, "Fred, I'll do just as I please,"
And the very next time I called I saw
That tuner still fingering the keys.
I said, "Get out," They said, "Get out yourself,"
And they meant it — for out of the place
I went with a foot (his or hers) in my back,
And the door was slammed in my face.

CHORUS.

4

I got over my folly, I courted again,
A bewitching but sensible maid,
But I went in for tuning, and in less than a month,
I was quite an adept at the trade.
Now we're married, and all my doubts and my fears
Are for evermore laid on the shelf,
For if ever her instrument gets out of tune,
I am able to tune it myself.

CHORUS.

WRITTEN & COMPOSED BY **T. HANLEY.** SUNG WITH THE GREATEST SUCCESS BY **SAM TORR.**

ENT. S. A. HALL

London: HOWARD & Co. 25, Great Marlborough Street, W.

Price 3/-

THE BULLS WON'T BELLOW.

WRITTEN AND COMPOSED BY T. HANLEY.

Moderato.

I used to be as hap_py as the lit_tle birds a_bove, As
live_ly as the lit_tle lambs at play, But
now I'm bro_ken-heart_ed, for I've lost the girl I love, With a
swell from town she's late_ly gone a_ _way. We

work'd up - on one farm, and my spirits she would charm, When
she would chant a pret - ty lit - tle song, But
e - ver since the day that my false love went a - way, The
farm, and all up - on it, has gone wrong.

CHORUS.
The bulls won't bellow, and the cows won't low, The hens won't cackle, and the
1st time p, 2nd f.
cocks won't crow, The turkeys won't gobble, and the ducks won't quack, And
ne-ver, ne-ver will do till my Jane comes back.
ff

2

There's something wrong with everything since Jane has gone away,
And I am doing nothing else but fret.
The cat with her back to the fire sits on the hearth all day,
And the poor old sheep - dog's nose is never wet.
The pigs won't curl their tails, the ducks won't eat the snails,
The gander now won't come home to be fed,
And the poor old Billy-goat has a big lump in his throat,
And a hogshead full of tears the sow has shed.

CHORUS.

3

The hens have got the whooping-cough, and will not leave their coop,
The canary is in the moult and will not eat,
The donkey's got bronchitis, and the tom-cat's got the croup,
The geese have all got chilblains in their feet.
The ferrets and the weasels are all down with the measles,
And all the wool is coming off the sheep,
The bull has got the tic, and the cow her calf won't lick,
And the horses have the night-mare when they sleep.

CHORUS.

4

To see the weeping willows, they all seem full of grief,
They seem to moan and shake their heads like me;
There's a sympathizing look on every cabbage leaf,
And a nod of pity, too, from every tree.
At night I dream of Jane, that she's come back again,
And I am whistling as I used to do,
But then when I awake, how I shiver and I shake,
When I find my dreams of pleasure are not true.

CHORUS

SUNG IN THE PRINCIPAL PANTOMIMES IN THE UNITED KINGDOM.

IN MY FUST 'USBANDS TIME

WRITTEN & COMPOSED BY

HARRY NICHOLLS,

SUNG WITH THE GREATEST SUCCESS BY

HERBERT CAMPBELL.

ENT. STA. HALL

Pr. 4/-

LONDON: HOPWOOD & CREW, 42, NEW BOND ST W.

STANNARD & SON.

IN MY FUST 'USBAND'S TIME.

Written and Composed by
HARRY NICHOLLS.

Arranged by
ERNEST J. SYMONS.

When I've cleaned myself and wash'd the kids, And go and fetch the beer, I
p
likes to have a friend_ly chat, And takes in all I hear, Oh!
laws a mus_sy me, I ses, To my neighbour Mis_sis Brown, How
things is chang_ing ev'_ry day, The world is up_side down...

CHORUS.
I think of the days as is gone for good, When a girl in my youth and
prime, I can see how dif_fer_ent things is now, Since
my first hus_band's time. I time......
1º
2º
f

1

When I've "cleaned" myself and wash'd the kids,
I go and fetch the beer,
I like to have a friendly chat,
And take in all I hear;
"Oh! laws a mussy me," I ses,
To my neighbour, Mrs Brown,
"How things is changing ev'ry day,
The world seems upside down!"
(*SPOKEN.*) *Yes, my dear, I says, things is changed since you and me was gals, But there, I says, I've nothing to grumble at. I've buried two, and I gets on very well with my third. But lor, I says, my dear, things is all topsey-turvey since you and me was gals—*

CHORUS.

And when I think of the days that's gone for good,
When a gal in my youth and prime,
I can see as things is different now,
Since *my* first husband's time!

2

We've only Coffee Taverns now,
When publics used to be,
And Music Halls you'll find will change,
For *beer* they'll give us *tea!*
The swells at the Theatres laugh,
At naughty jokes they hear,
But them same jokes is wicked,
Where there's smoke and drinking beer!
(*SPOKEN.*) *Yes, my dear, I says, what's wicked on one side of the road appears very respectable on the other. It's all according to the people who patronize it. I'm sure, me and him went to the play the other night, and it was shameful to see them gals a dancing and a jigging about the stage without anything on to speak of, some of them, I says, I suppose you call this Art, don't you? He says, "Yes!" my dear, he says it's quite too constummick! "Yes" I says, "and quite too everything else as far as I can see!" But then, my dear, things is altered since you and me was gals—*

CHORUS.

For whenever we went to a play, my dear,
Or to see a Pantomime,
The girls didn't throw there legs so high,
Not in my first husband's time.

3

We all go in for *Art*, my dear,
To do things wrong we're taught,
For the gents all lets their hair grow long,
While the ladies cut theirs short!
We sprawl upon the floor instead,
Of sitting on our chairs,
At sunflowers, dado's, chaney-pots,
We gaze with vacant stare.
(*SPOKEN.*) *There's that Miss Snaggs, she was took "intense" all of a sudden, and said she wanted a "Dado." We tried to reason her out of it, but she would have it, and now she's more than too utterly quite, And serve her right too, Fancy a woman at her time of life wanting a "Dado." I'm sure when you and me was gals, my dear, we didn't want no "Dado's." But there, my dear, things is altered since you and me was gals—*

CHORUS.

For we didn't think an old cracked pot "intense,"
Nor an old blue plate "sublime,"
For things as a rule was "blue" enough,
In *my* first husband's time.

4

The good old day's departed now,
When England's name was feared,
Those glories won by field and flood,
For ever disappeared;
We make our soldiers playthings now,
All thirst for glory's vain,
For we send them out to face the foe,
And call them back again.
(*SPOKEN.*) *Yes, I'm sure it's something sickening the way they treat our soldiers now. A parcel of old women in Parliament, what do I say? old women? ah! perhaps if some of us old women was sent there, we wouldn't give way to nobody, whether we was right or wrong. Did you ever know a woman who did? But there, my dear, as I says, things is changed since you and me was gals—*

CHORUS.

For when our soldiers went to fight for us,
In a far-off distant clime,
They didn't come back without having a "go,"
Not in *my* first husband's time.

5

Religion now is all a farce,
We're in a pretty plight—
When pious rogues—converted thieves,
Can teach us what is right;
With shrieks and yells and blasphemies,
And language most profane,
We're told that in another world,
We all shall meet again!
(*SPOKEN.*) *It will be a nice place to go to, with some of those gentlemen about, won't it? If this is the sort of company we're to mix with hereafter, I'll be content with a back seat where I can see just as well. But there, my dear, things is altered since you and me was gals—*

CHORUS.

For we didn't have a sermon preach'd in slang,
Nor a hymn like a comic rhyme,
And we didn't want to stand on our heads to pray,
Not in *my* first husband's time!

6

In days gone by, good *honest men*,
Would fight their country's cause,
Not rob the poor in Freedom's name,
Nor live for mere applause;
Afraid to strike the blow at first,
To make these Traitors quail,
We wait until the mischief's done,
Then clap them into jail!
(*SPOKEN.*) *A lot of good it will do now, won't it. Ah! my dear, I don't want to name no names, but if somebody I could mention was alive now, this game would have been stopped long ago. But, you see, my dear, it's all altered since you and me was gals—*

CHORUS.

If a man really worked for his country's good,
Up the ladder of fame he'd climb,
But it wasn't by treason that the trick was done,
Not in *my* first husband's time!

H & C

UP WENT THE PRICE

WRITTEN & COMPOSED BY

GEORGE WARE,

SUNG WITH IMMENSE SUCCESS

BY

G. H. MACDERMOTT.

ENT. STA. HALL.

Pr. 4/.

LONDON: HOPWOOD & CREW, 42, NEW BOND ST. W.

UP WENT THE PRICE.

Written and Composed by
GEORGE WARE

Arranged by
ERNEST J. SYMONS.

I find it hard, ve--ry, ve--ry hard, Tho'
ev'--ry means I try......... My
liv_ing to get, and keep out of debt, But I
can't and I don't know why........ I

bought a butch- - er's shop last year A

grand one in High Street . . . . . . Oh!

dear, oh, dear! it turned out queer,

Up went the price of meat . . . .

CHORUS.
Up went the price of meat . . . . Up went the price of
meat . . . . . There's heaps of trouble on this young man's mind They
raised the price of meat . . . . .
meat . . . .
1º
2º
f
f

1

I find it hard very, very hard though every means I try,
My living to get and keep out of debt, but I can't and I don't know why,
I bought a Butcher's shop last year, a grand one in High Street,
Oh! dear, oh! dear, it turned out queer, up went the price of meat.

CHORUS.

Up went the price of meat, up went the price of meat,
There's heaps of troubles on this young man's mind, they raised the price of meat!

2

I sold that shop and another one took, but very much against my wish,
To deal out pickled eels and whelks, dried cod, and hot fried fish,
But it wouldn't sell, and oh! such a smell, arose from the whelks in the dish,
The fishermen struck my usual luck, up went the price of fish.
(*Chorus.*) Up went the price, &c.

3

I sold that shop and another one took, with a license to deal in game,
Bad luck to the man who sold me that shop it's enough to turn my brain,
A collision on the Eastern line broke up the poultry trucks,
Oh! dear, oh! lor, I believe I swore, up went the price of ducks.
(*Chorus.*) Up went the price, &c.

4

I sold that shop and another one took, but quite in a differant line,
But things went wrong I couldn't get along, the cause I will assign,
'Twas a greengrocer's shop, and I bought all the lot, of baskets and weighing machines,
But it wouldn't pay, for the very next day, up went the price of greens.
(*Chorus.*) Up went the price, &c.

5

I sold that shop and another one took, in the oil and colour line,
With pickles jam and marmalade, soft soap, and balls of twine,
'Twas another sell, for I know very well, they had me for a lamb,
The market rose and as you may suppose, up went the price of jam.
(*Chorus.*) Up went the price, &c.

6

I sold that shop and wouldn't take another, but thought I'd take a wife,
I'd lost my money and wanted some more, and was tired of single life,
But the Dutch sent over a shipload of Counts, and Scotland a cartload of Earls,
They got the run of the market first, so up went the price of the girls.
(*Chorus.*) Up went the price, &c.

H & C. 2315.

Berridge, Bros. Engravers & Steam Lithos.

BAA BAA BAA

COMIC SONG.

STANNARD & SON

SUNG WITH IMMENSE SUCCESS BY

JOLLY NASH.

WRITTEN BY

WALTER GREENAWAY.

MUSIC BY

VINCENT DAVIES.

ENT. STA. HALL.

LONDON: HOPWOOD & CREW, 42, NEW BOND ST. W.

Pr. 4/.

BAA! BAA! BAA!

or

THE LAWYER AND THE SHEEP STEALER.

Written by
WALTER GREENAWAY.

Composed by
VINCENT DAVIES.

cun_ning old law_yer came to him one day To pay him his price the
man did a_gree Says the law_yer I'll tell you now how to get free You must
look at the Judge in a soft va_cant way_ And when he speaks to you look
sil_ _ _ly and say, Baa! baa! baa! . . . . . .
ff

Said the man with a grin when the plan he did hear, Trust me I'll look silly enough ne_ver fear, I'll
p
make t'owd Judge rayther o_pen his eyes, And the Ju_ry_men all scratch their yeds in surprise, All
right said the Lawyer and thought of his fee, You will play out your part ve_ry well I can see And the
jailors all wondered and couldn't tell why For all night they thought they could hear a sheep cry.
Baa! baa! baa! . . .
ff

1

I'll sing you a story, which p'r'aps you all know,
About the sheepstealer a long time ago,
Who was caught in the act, and in prison he lay,
When a cunning old lawyer came to him one day;
To pay him his price the man did agree,
Says the lawyer I'll tell you now how to get free,
You must look at the Judge in a soft vacant way,
And when he speaks to you, look silly and say—
Baa! baa! *baa!*

2

Said the man with a grin, when the plan he did hear,
Trust me I'll look silly enough, never fear,
I'll make t'owd Judge rayther open his eyes,
And the Jurymen all scratch their yeds in surprise;
All right said the lawyer, and thought of his fee,
You will play your part very well I can see,
And the jailors all wondered, and couldn't tell why,
For all night they thought they could hear a sheep cry—
Baa! baa! *baa!*

3

The next day was fixed for his trial to take place,
He soon was found guilty, 'twas such a clear case,
So silence was called, not a sound could you hear,
As the Judge began speaking in tones so severe,
Prisoner, you see what you've come to at last,
What have you to say before sentence is passed,
But the prisoner who stood slowly wagging his head,
Just looked at the Judge very silly, and said—
Baa! baa! *baa!*

4

There was a tremendous commotion in court,
The prisoner was silly, so every one thought,
And the jailors declared he could not be right,
For they swore he had baa'd like a sheep all the night,
Said the Judge the poor man is a fool I can see,
He must be discharged, so let him go free,
And the prisoner who stood looking round him so shy,
As they led him away began loudly to cry—
Baa! baa! *baa!*

5

When he got outside the old lawyer was there,
Ha, bravo! said he, you did well I declare,
From laughing I hardly knew how to refrain,
But don't let them catch you at that game again;
Now as I'm in a hurry to get off you see,
Just be quick as you can and hand over my fee,
But the man stood and looked in a most silly way,
Grinned at the old lawyer, and slyly did say—
Baa! baa! *baa!*

HENRI CLARK'S GREAT SONG.

SHE DOES THE FANDANGO ALL OVER THE PLACE

WRITTEN & COMPOSED BY

G. W. HUNT

ENT. STA. HALL.

Pr. 4/-

LONDON: HOPWOOD & CREW, 42, NEW BOND ST W.

SHE DOES THE FANDANGO ALL OVER THE PLACE.

Written and Composed by
G. W. HUNT.

Arranged by
ERNEST J. SYMONS.

I've seen ma - ny beau - ties, Whilst trav'-ling a - - round The
world, but in Spain, There my fan - - cy I found, She'd
hair black as coal, Eyes bright as a star, And I
felt fair - - ly gone, As she twang'd her gui - - tar.

CHORUS.
She sang like a night-in-gale, twang'd the gui-tar, Danced the Ca-chu--ca, and smokes a ci--gar, O! what a form, O! what a face, And she done the Fan-dan-go all o-ver the place.
Sym.

1

I've seen many beauties,
Whilst travelling around
The world, but in Spain,
There my fancy I found;
She'd hair black as coal,
Eyes bright as a star,
And I felt fairly gone,
As she twanged her guitar!

(*Cho*s.) She sang like a nightingale, twanged the guitar,
Danced the Cachuca, and smoked a cigar,
O! what a form, O! what a face!
And she did the Fandango, all over the place.

2

She'd sing me the songs,
Of her sweet sunny land,
Altho' what about
I could ne'er understand;
I tried to explain,
That my heart was a flame,
And if eyes could express,
She felt slightly the same.

(SPOKEN.) On being introduced to her father, a villainous looking personage, he said something like this, "Hah! Sostenuto! Allegretto! Cigaretto!" I said, "my dear sir, you are quite right in your observation" there was something wrong somewhere, for he flourished a dagger and said, Ho! Da Capo, Bodega, "Intimidado," so to soothe him —

(*Cho*s.) — She sang, &c.

3

To England I brought her,
To make her my bride,
And when my friends saw her,
They laughed till they cried;
And the buttons flew off
From a dozen white vests,
When at breakfast she somewhat
Astonished the guest.

(*Cho*s.) And sang, &c.

4

But she carries her Spanish ways,
Slightly too far,
I at times think I'll have
To destroy that guitar;
For she sits at the window,
And sings long and loud,
Until in the street
She collects a large crowd,

(SPOKEN.) And horrid boys cry out, "chuck it out, Sarah," dreadful, and when I insist on her concluding her performance, she rushes into the garden, mounts the summer house, and won't come down till she's —

(*Cho*s.) Sang like a nightingale, twanged the guitar,
Danced the Cachuca, and smoked a cigar,
Devilish bad form, quite a disgrace,
She *will* do the Fandango all over the place.

THIS IS THE HOUSE THAT JERRY BUILT

SUNG WITH
ENORMOUS SUCCESS BY
JAMES FAWN.

WRITTEN BY
T. S. LONSDALE.

COMPOSED BY
W. G. EATON.

ENT. STA. HALL.

Pr. 4/.

LONDON. HOPWOOD & CREW, 42, NEW BOND ST W.

THIS IS THE HOUSE THAT JERRY BUILT.

Written by T. S. LONSDALE.

Composed by W. G. EATON.

My wife is a wo_man and like all the rest,
p
Bound to be scheming, some_thing for the best, She
had a de_ _sire a few months a_ _go, To
live in the suburbs of Lon_don you know, She

went out in search, and ve_-_ry soon found, An

a_-_gent who show'd her the houses all round, They

set_tled on one af_-_ter a good hunt, In

the Go_thic style and a gar_-_den in front.

CHORUS.
And there's the cat, that eat the rat, and the servant girl's not fat, And there's the
children with the cramp, Because the place is al_ways damp, And there's the
work_man al_ways nigh, and the plum_ber al_ways dry, And
thro' the roof you see the sky in the house that Jerry built, And there's the
1º
2º
house that Jerry built.
f

1

My wife is a woman, and like all the rest,
Bound to be scheming something for the best,
She had a desire a few months ago,
To live in the suburbs of London you know;
She went out in search and very soon found,
An Agent who showed her the houses all round,
They settled on one, after a good hunt,
In the Gothic style – and a garden in front.

(SPOKEN.) And also a pond in front, I should have said, for the road was nothing better, when the men brought the furniture, they were up to here in mud and it took them a day and a half to dig the Van out of the road, and the mould in the garden is mould, I put in some seeds a few months ago, all that came up were half bricks and clay –

CHORUS.

And there's the cat that eat the rat,
And the servant girl's not fat,
And there's the children with the cramp,
Because the place is always damp.
And there's the workman always nigh,
And the Plumber always dry,
And through the roof, you see the sky,
In the house that Jerry built.

2

Red bricks and church windows look very nice,
And the place some might think is a paradise,
Other sweet things in the Gothic style but,
The doors like the windows will never quite shut.
If the wind's the wrong way, it's really no joke,
We're smothered to death with volumes of smoke,
But there we all sit and shiver with cold,
Or up in some shawls or blankets we're rolled.

(SPOKEN.) Can't have a fire in the place because the chimney smokes, oh it is a nice place to live in, the nearest Pub's a mile off, when the girl goes for the supper beer, we bid her good-bye, just the same as if she was off to America, and perhaps I'm dying of thirst, or the Missus or children has got the wind or spasms bad, and want a drop of short to keep us warm, you-know – (*Chorus.*)

3

It's nice don't you know, at night when in bed,
For the rain to come through and drop on your head,
And the wife of your buzzum to sit up and jaw,
While you rush about, and wipe up the floor.
Another nice thing that worries your brains,
Is the whistle that's from a few passing trains,
An old cock that crows will give you delight,
And also a dog that howls half the night.

(SPOKEN.) They say when you hear a dog howl its a sign of *death*, the next morning to the *Dog*, oh it is a nice place to live in, we can never get a girl to stay longer than a month, because the place is so dull, and no Soldiers about, Policemen you see once a week, and Burglars every night, it's a good place for Doctors and Dentists, some one's always got the toothache, whooping cough or measles – (*Chorus.*)

4

Through the walls you can hear what your neighbours say,
And when they commence the piano to play
The five finger exercise, and other sweet things,
A Cornet sometimes a friend of theirs brings,
You feel just as if, you could tear out your hair,
Or at your dear wife you could say a sweet prayer,
For she, yes, the woman's the cause of it all,
When the water taps froze and the children squall.

(SPOKEN.) The wife says, oh yes its all my fault you blame me, for every thing, I'm the cause of it all you strike me, now do, do it! or say I'm mad, and have me put away, because I took this beastly house and think a Donkey's got a soul, one husband's done it to his wife, but he's been well done since –

(*Chorus.*)

THE SUCCESS OF THE GAIETY BURLESQUE "MAZEPPA"
WAS MISS BESSIE BELLWOOD'S SONG "WHAT CHEER 'RIA"
SUNG BY MISS NELLY FARREN. Vide Press.

"WHAT CHEER 'RIA"

STANNARD & SON.

WRITTEN BY

WILL HERBERT

COMPOSED & SUNG WITH ENORMOUS SUCCESS BY

BESSIE BELLWOOD.

PROFESSIONAL VOCALISTS MAY NOT SING THIS SONG IN PUBLIC WITHOUT MISS BESSIE BELLWOOD'S PERMISSION.

ENT. STA. HALL.

LONDON: HOPWOOD & CREW, 42, NEW BOND ST W.

Pr. 4/-

WHAT CHEER 'RIA.

Written by WILL HERBERT. Composed by Miss BESSIE BELLWOOD.

Arranged by GEO. ISON.

I am a girl what's a doing wery well in the weagetable line, And
as I'd sav'd a bob or two I thought I'd cut a shine, So I
goes and buys some tog_ge_ry, these ere wery clothes you see, And
with the money I had left I thought I'd have a spree. So I

goes in-to a music hall where I'd of-ten been a-fore, I
don't go in the gal-le-ry, but on the bottom floor, I
sits down by the Chairman, and calls for a pot of Stout, My
pals in the gallery spotted me, and they all commenc'd to shout—

CHORUS.
What cheer Ri_a? Ri_a's on the job, What cheer
2nd time 8va.
Ri_a? did you speculate a bob, Oh, Ri_a she's a toff, and she
looks immen_si_koff, And they all shouted "what cheer
1º
Ri_a?".
2º
Ri_a?"
Sym.

1

I am a girl what's a-doing wery well in the weagetable line,
And as I'd saved a bob or two, I thought I'd cut a shine;
So I goes and buys some toggery, these ere wery clothes you see,
And with the money I had left, I thought I'd have a spree:
So I goes into a Music Hall, where I'd often been afore,
I don't go in the gallery, but on the bottom floor;
I sits down by the Chairman, and calls for a pot of stout,
My pals in the gallery, spotted me, and they all commenced to shout —

CHORUS.

What cheer Ria! Ria's on the job,
What cheer Ria! did you speculate a bob?
Oh Ria she's a toff and she looks immensikoff,
And they all shouted "What cheer Ria!"

2

Of course I chaffed them back again, but it worn't a bit of use,
The poor old Chairman's baldie head, they treated with abuse;
They threw an orange down at me, it went bang inside a pot,
The beer went up like a fountain, and a toff copt all the lot:
It went slap in his chevey, and it made an awful mess,
But what gave me the needle was, it spoilt my blooming dress;
I thought it was getting rather warm, so I goes towards the door,
When a man shoves out his gammy leg, and I fell smack on the floor.

(SPOKEN.) I turned round and spoke to him wery politely, — I said, What cher want to go and shove your jolly old gammy leg out like that for? He said, I beg your pardon Madam, I says, beg nothing; you jolly old Josser! He says, Don't you be saucy or I shall get you chucked out, When my pals spot I'm having a row, and they see the old man has got a wooden leg, They shout out, What yer! "Half a man and half a tree!"

(*Chorus.*) What cheer Ria! &c.

3

Now the gent that keeps the Music Hall he patters to the bloke,
Of course they blamed it all on me, but I couldn't see the joke;
So I up'd and told the govenor as how he'd shoved me down,
And with his jolly old wooden leg, tore the frilling off my gown:
But law bless you! it worn't a bit of use, the toff was on the job,
They said outside! and out I went, and they stuck to my bob;
Of course I felt so wild, to think how I'd been taken down,
Next time I'll go in the gallery with my pals, you bet a crown.

(SPOKEN.) You don't catch me going chucking my money away, trying to be a toff any more, The way they served me wasn't so wery polite, They brought the 'Chucker out' and he said, Come on Ria, you've been kicking up a pretty row, he says, Come on outside, I says Shan't! shan't!! there you are! Shant! He took hold of me and handed me out, just as though I'd been a sack o' taters. When I got outside, my young man was outside, So he says, Serves you jolly well right Ria! You shouldn't try to be a lady, 'caus it don't suit yer, Just then my pals were coming out of the gallery, and they all commenced shouting —

(*Chorus.*) What cheer Ria! &c.

THE BOY IN THE GALLERY

WRITTEN & COMPOSED BY

GEORGE WARE,

SUNG WITH THE GREATEST SUCCESS BY

NELLY POWER.

ENT. STA. HALL. Pr. 4/-

LONDON: HOPWOOD & CREW, 42, NEW BOND ST W.

THE BOY IN THE GALLERY.

Written and Composed by GEORGE WARE.

I'm a young girl and have just come o - ver,
p
O - ver from the Coun - try where they do things big,
And amongst the boys I've got a lov - er, And
since I've got a lov - er why I don't care a fig.

CHORUS.
The boy I love is up in the gal_ler_y, The boy I love is
looking now at me, There he is can't you see wa_ving his handkerchief As
merry as a Ro_bin that sings on a tree.
DANCE.
f

1

I'm a young girl and have just come over,
Over from the country where they do things big;
And amongst the boys I've got a lover,
And since I've got a lover, why I don't care a fig!

CHORUS.

The boy I love is up in the gallery,
The boy I love is looking now at me;
There he is can't you see? waving his handkerchief,
As merry as a robin that sings on the tree.

2

The boy that I love they call him a cobler,
But he's not a cobler, allow me to state;
For Johnny is a tradesman, and he works in the Boro',
Where they sole and heel them whilst you wait.
(Chorus.) The boy I love, &c.

3

Now if I were a Duchess and had a lot of money,
I'd give it to the boy that's going to marry me;
But I hav'n't got a penny so we'll live on love and kisses,
And be just as happy as the birds on the tree.
(Chorus.) The boy I love, &c.

FUNNY THINGS THEY DO UPON THE SLY.

WRITTEN BY

G.W. HUNTER, AND JOHN COOKE JUN[R].

COMPOSED & SUNG WITH IMMENSE SUCCESS

BY

G.W. HUNTER.

ENT. STA. HALL.

PRICE 4/-

LONDON; HOPWOOD & CREW, 42, NEW BOND STREET. W.

FUNNY THINGS THEY DO UPON THE SLY.

Written by
G.W. HUNTER & JOHN COOKE Jun.r

Composed by
G.W. HUNTER.

A - dam and Eve were simple in their way, Like a
p
pair of lit - tle kit - tens, so they say, Wore
nothing but their skins, From their heads down to their shins, And
walk'd a - round the gar - den all the day, Though

strangers to each o-ther at the start, They be-
-gan to love each o-ther by and by, And
e-ver since that day, The divil has been to pay, Such
fun-ny things are done up-on the sly. So if you'll

lend me your at - ten - tion for a while, To a -
- muse you a lit - tle I will try, I'll
not de - tain you long, And I'll tell you in my song, Some
fun - ny things they do up - on the sly.
f

1

Adam and Eve were simple in their way,
Like a pair of little kittens, so they say,
Wore nothing but their skins,
From their heads down to their shins,
And walked around the garden all the day:
Though strangers to each other at the start,
They began to love each other by-and-bye,
And ever since that day,
The devil has been to pay,
Such funny things are done upon the sly;
So if you'll lend me your attention for a while,
To amuse you a little I will try,
I'll not detain you long,
And I'll tell you in my song,
Some funny things they do upon the sly.

2

There's the giddy little maiden, full of gush,
She's pretty, but her head is soft as mush,
Of course she's got a 'mash',
With a very sick moustache,
On thirty bob a week he's very flush;
He flirts with every pretty little miss,
And gives each one a sugar-coated kiss,
Says, "good-bye at the gate,
It's getting rather late,"
But to meet another girl it is his wish:
He takes her to a Party or a Ball,
He tells her that he'll wed her by-and-bye:
But the neighbours wink and say,
In a very knowing way,
"Some funny things are done upon the sly."

3

There's the slavey who pretends to be devout,
Who every other night wants to go out,
"To a *Meeting*" she will say,
But it's always to the Play,
With a fellow who will stand her bottled stout;
There's the lonely widow, smiling very sweet,
Who dresses very charmingly and neat,
In company it's the plan,
When addressed by a man,
To blush from her eyebrows to her feet;
But let her catch a "jay" when he's alone,
He'll find her not so bashful or so shy,
That's laid upon the shelf,
You know how 'tis yourself,
Such funny things are done upon the sly.

4

There's the Parson who's supposed to be so good,
Do wrong you'd really think he never could,
But now and then we read,
Of some very funny deed,
That a Parson's done, but which he never should;
There's the stiff old maid, who likes to fume and boil,
She's been made so long, she's very apt to spoil,
Secretly she'll plan,
To try and trap a man,
She's equal to a dose of castor oil:
If she could grab a man and lock him up,
When not another living soul was nigh,
She'd take away his breath,
She'd squeeze the man to death,
Such funny things are done upon the sly.

5

There's the bachelor who looks so very slow,
As if unto a goose he can't say "Bo,"
But though he looks so shy,
He can wink a wicked eye,
And it's not worth knowing what *he* doesn't know;
And the married man who goes around at night,
On the spree and then goes home so jolly tight,
Says, he was at the Lodge,
When a poker he will dodge,
His wife gets out of bed and wants to fight,
She suspects that he's been out with the girls,
There's a hair upon his coat, he can't deny,
It's a pretty piece of 'biz',
But you know how it is,
Such funny things are done upon the sly.

BERRIDGE, BROS ENGRAVERS & PRINTERS

STANNARD & SON, IMPᵗ

ANGELS WITHOUT WINGS.

Written and Composed by
GEO. DANCE.

Arranged by
GEO. LE BRUNN.

The la_dies heaven bless them, now we love them ev'_ry one, We
praise them and we toast them o'er our wine . . . . . . We
laud their ma_ny virtues and we sound their ma_ny deeds, And
call them dar_ling an_gels so di_ _vine . . . . But
p

may be, at the time the lit_tle husseys are at home,
Pen_cil_ing their eye_brows with_out shame....... Their
blushes as di_vine are ten to one car_mine, But
still we call them an_gels just the same........

CHORUS Tempo di Valse.

1

The ladies heaven bless them, we love them every one,
We praise them and we toast them o'er our wine;
We laud their many virtues and we sound their many deeds,
And call them darling angels so divine:
But may be at the time, the little husseys are at home,
Pencilling their eyebrows without shame;
Their blushes so divine are ten to one carmine,
But still we call them angels just the same.

CHORUS.

Angels, angels, angels without wings,
Simple, very simple, very pious little things,
Angels, angels floating all about,
Like the men, you're angels, when you're not found out.

2

Our angels love enjoyment and we take them up and down,
Of course that is the duty of the men;
And though celestial creatures are supposed to live on air,
They relish stout and oysters now and then:
We often buy the darlings gloves and when we ask the size,
They vow that they wear sixes with great ease,
And they take 'em back next day, and to the shopman say
I'll have three sizes larger if you please.
(*Chorus.*) Angels, angels, angels, &c.

3

As time goes on we wed them, these darlings without wings,
And call them ever after darling wife;
They darn up all our stockings and they make our buttons fast,
And comfort and console us throughout life:
But if our health's declining they persuade us make our wills,
Of course we leave them all that we possess,
And when we are no more, the widower next door,
Proposes and our angel answers "yes!"
(*Chorus.*) Angels, angels, angels, &c.

TI! HI! TIDDELLY HI!

WRITTEN AND COMPOSED BY

JOSEPH TABRAR

AND THE SINGER IS SAVED! SAVED!! SAVED!!!

SUNG WITH IMMENSE SUCCESS BY

HARRY RICKARDS.

H. G. BANKS LITH

ENT. STA. HALL.

PR 4/-

LONDON:
HOPWOOD & CREW, 42, NEW BOND STREET. W.

STANNARD & SON.

TI! HI! TIDDELLY HI!

Written and Composed by JOSEPH TABRAR.

Songs! oh, songs, could I but find 'em, Where can good song
wri-ters be? Would! oh, would I were be-hind 'em,
I'd pay them to write for me, Fame, great fame, the
way to win is, Don't be-grudge a de-cent sum;

But plank down your mer - ry gui_neas, And suc_cess is

sure to come. I've tried hard to find a dit_ _ty,

That would not turn out a_ _miss; Some young fel_ _low

in the Ci_ty, One day last week sent me this.

CHORUS. ALLEGRO.
Ti! Hi! Tiddel-ly, Hi! that's the way the tune goes.
Ti! Hi Tiddelly, Hi! Pom' pom' pom'.... Ti! Hi!
Tiddel-ly, Hi! that's the way the words go; Is-n't it a
won-der where the songs come from?... from....
1º
2º

1

Songs! oh, songs, could I but find 'em,
Where can good song writers be?
Would! oh, would I were behind 'em,
I'd pay them to write for me.
Fame, great fame, the way to win is,
Don't begrudge a decent sum;
But plank down your merry guineas,
And success is sure to come.
I've tried hard to find a ditty,
That would not turn out amiss;
Some young fellow in the City,
One day last week sent me this.

3

His third verse is blythe and merry,
Every line is most serene,
Quoting Churchill, Lord Salis-bury,
Prince of Wales, Princess and Queen.
Every subject that is Royal
He speaks of in joyous tones,
Making every sentence Loyal
To all monarchs and all thrones.
There's supposed to be a party,
All is pleasure, mirth, and bliss;
Everybody's laughing hearty,
While the Queen is singing this.

CHORUS.

Ti! Hi! Tiddelly, Hi! that's the way the tune goes.
Ti! Hi! Tiddelly, Hi! Pom' pom' pom'.
Ti! Hi! Tiddelly, Hi! that's the way the words go;
Isn't it a wonder where the songs come from.

2

In his second verse he mentions,
Give a cheer for Charles Bradlaugh;
Stop at once Perpetual Pensions,
Think of London's Starving Poor.
There's a story and its sequel,
Worked out on an excellent plan;
And he calls it, "Who can equal,"
William G. the "Grand Old Man."
Then he lays a verse before us,
With its thesis well revealed;
Singing this Chaotic Chorus,
After praising Beaconsfield.
(Chorus.) Ti! Hi! Tiddelly, Hi! &c.

4

I might almost say I know it's
Bound to be a big success,
Though I seldom praise my poets,
In this case I can't do less.
He brings in such spicy topics,
And some *lines* about as warm
As you'd find *lines* in the tropics,
Placed in metaphoric form.
On next Monday night I'll sing it,
Hoping it will prove a go,
But before intact I bring it,
Just let's hear how much you know.
(Chorus.) Ti! Hi! Tiddelly, Hi! &c.

This Song may be Sung in Public without fee or Licence, Except at Theatres or Music Halls.
"BUY ME SOME ALMOND ROCK."
SAY YOU'LL BE MINE & I'LL RENOUNCE EVERY-THING EVEN MY HOME-RULE BILL
THE G.O.M GETS EXCITED.
A NICE CUP OF TEA WITH "LABBY."
PURE SWEETS 8D PER OUNCE
NFECTIO
WRITTEN AND COMPOSED BY
JOSEPH TABRAR.
SUNG BY
MISS MARIE LLOYD.
RANDY PANDY WAITS ON ME WITH SUGAR-DE-CANDY.
Copyright.
Price 4/-
LONDON,
HOPWOOD & CREW, 42, NEW BOND STREET, W.

BUY ME SOME ALMOND ROCK.

Written and Composed by JOSEPH TABRAR.

I feel so glad, I ne-ver had Such joy with-in my heart, I've
been ask'd out, and with-out doubt I'm dying to make a start; I've
ne-ver seen a ball, nor been Al-low'd out af-ter dark, I'll
mash the men, nine out of-ten, Oh won't it be a lark....

CHORUS.

On - - ly fancy if Gladstone's there, And falls in love with me.....
If I run across La - bou - chere I'll ask him home to tea......
I shall say to a young man gay If he treads up - on my frock.....
Randy pan - dy sugardy candy Buy me some Almond Rock...
Rock...

Sung by MARIE LLOYD.

BUY ME SOME ALMOND ROCK.

Written and Composed by JOSEPH TABRAR.

1

I feel so glad, I never had
Such joy within my heart;
I've been asked out, and without doubt
I'm dying to make a start.
I've never seen a ball, nor been
Allowed out after dark,
I'll mash the men, nine out of ten,
Oh! wont it be a lark.

CHORUS.

Only fancy if Gladstone's there,
And falls in love with me,
If I run across Labouchere,
I'll ask him home to tea.
I shall say to a young man gay,
If he treads upon my frock,
Randy pandy, sugardy candy,
Buy me some Almond Rock.

2

I heard in truth that General Booth
Is going to be M. C.,
And if he is, 'twill be good "biz,"
No end of fun there'll be.
Ma said last week, I'm not to speak
To even one young man,
But just you wait, in spite of fate,
I'll speak to all I can.
(Chorus.) Only fancy, &c.

3

If Sir Charles Dilke sees me in silk,
To dance with me he'll try,
I'll sing "Tral la" Ha! "There you are"
Then "Wink the other eye."
If by a "fluke" I meet a Duke,
A Marquis or an Earl,
I'll win all three, in fact I'll be
A regular "Giddy girl."
(Chorus.) Only fancy, &c.

This Song may be Sung in Public without Fee or Licence, Except at Music Halls.

OH! M^R. PORTER.

WRITTEN BY THOMAS LE BRUNN. COMPOSED BY GEORGE LE BRUNN.

Came up to see the wond'rous sights of famous Lon_don Town.......
Just a week I had of it, all round the place we'd roam ......
Was_n't I sor_ry on the day I had to go back home?.....
Worried a_bout with pack_ing, I ar_rived late at the sta_tion,

Dropped my hat - box in the mud, the things all fell a -
bout,
Got my tick - et, said 'good - bye,'
Right a - way!" the guard did cry,
But I found the
train was wrong, and shout - ed out;

CHORUS.
Oh! Mister Por - ter, what shall I do?........ I want to go to
Birmingham and they're taking me on to Crewe. Send me back to Lon - don as
quickly as you can,........ Oh! Mis - ter Porter, what a sil - ly girl I
1st time.
2nd time.
am.
am......

Lately I just spent a week with my old Aunt Brown,
Came up to see the wond'rous sights of famous London Town.
Just a week I had of it, all round the place I'd roam,
Wasn't I sorry on the day I had to go back home.
Worried about with packing, we arrived late at the station
Dropped my hat-box in the mud, the things all fell about
Got my ticket, said good-bye, "Right away!" the guard did cry,
But I found the train was wrong and shouted out :—

Oh! Mr. Porter, what shall I do?
I want to go to Birmingham and they're taking me on to Crewe,
Send me back to London as quickly as you can,
Oh! Mr. Porter, what a silly girl I am.

The porter would not stop the train, but laughed and said "You must
Keep your hair on, Mary Ann, and mind that you don't bust!"
Some old gentleman inside declared that it was hard,
Said "Look out of the window, Miss, and try and call the guard."
Didn't I, too, with all my might I nearly balanced over,
But my old friend grasped my leg, and pulled me back again,
Nearly fainting with the fright, I sank into his arms a sight,
Went into hysterics but I cried in vain :—

(CHORUS.)

On his clean old shirt front then I laid my trembling head,
"Do take it easy, rest awhile," the dear old chappie said.
If you make a fuss of me and on me do not frown,
You shall have my mansion, dear, away in London town.
Wouldn't you think me silly if I said I could not like him?
Really he seemed a nice old boy, so I replied this way;
I will be your own for life your imay doodleum little wife.
If you'll never tease me any more I say.

(CHORUS.)

This Song may be Sung in Public without Fee or Licence, Except at Music Halls.

So Her Sister Says.

SHE'S A MILLINER. (SO HER SISTER SAYS.)

H.G. BANKS LITH.

SHE GOT SPLICED THIS AFTERNOON AND, — WELL, IT WASN'T MUCH TOO SOON. SO THE LADY IN THE FIRST FLOOR BACK SAYS.

Written By
JOHN P. HARRINGTON,
Composed by GEO. LE BRUNN,
Sung By
MISS JENNY
VALMORE.

Price 4/-

LONDON;
HOPWOOD & CREW, 42 NEW BOND STREET, W.
H.G. BANKS imp^t

SO HER SISTER SAYS.

Written by J. P. HARRINGTON. Composed by GEO. LE BRUNN.

Arranged by EZRA READ.

A girl who lives just op-po-site, I wish it un-der-stood, Has
p
proved a per-fect mys-te-ry to all our neighbour-hood; Her
brother, and her married Sis, live in the house, with her, She's
out all day, from ear-ly morn, And she's a mil-lin-er.

CHORUS.
So her sis-ter says! Her married sis-ter says! And
2nd time f
so, like--wise, her bro-ther Jack says: Well, she
may be one, it's true, But still it keeps her out till two– So the
la-dy in the first-floor back says! So the back says!
1º
2º
p
ff

SO HER SISTER SAYS.

Written by J. P. HARRINGTON. Composed by GEO. LE BRUNN.

1.

A girl who lives just opposite, I wish it understood,
Has proved a perfect mystery to all our neighbourhood;
Her brother, and her married Sis, live in the house, with her,
She's out all day, from early morn, and she's a milliner.

CHORUS.

So her *sister* says! Her married *sister* says!
And so, likewise, her brother Jack says!
Well, she *may* be one, it's true,
But still it keeps her out till two—
So the lady in the first-floor back says!

2.

I passed their street-door late one night, and what should you suppose?
Saw Mrs Johnson's husband kiss that girl beneath the nose;
I certainly *will* own 'twas dark, no moon about, you know,
And Mary Ann somehow mistook old Johnson for her beau—

CHORUS.

So her sister says! Her married *sister* says!
And so, likewise, her brother Jack says!
But that tricky Mary Ann
Has done the same with *her* old man,
So the lady in the first-floor back says!

3.

She's fond of balls, and parties too, that young girl opposite,
She's always out at dances, and they last half through the night;
One week, she hired a special cab, came out dressed up in state,
She went to Covent Garden Ball, and came home *rather* late—

CHORUS.

So her *sister* says! Her married sister says!
And so, likewise, her brother Jack says!
Must have stopped to make a call,
'Cos—here!—She didn't get home at all—
So the lady in the first-floor back says!

4.

She's not so young as she looks, though she makes up very well,
Some say she's half-past thirty, but of course that's hard to tell;
When we heard she'd got married, we could hardly keep in bounds,
To-day she wed a gentleman with thirty thousand pounds.

CHORUS.

So her *sister* says! Her *married* sister says!
And so, likewise, her brother Jack says!
She got spliced this afternoon,
And—well, it wasn't much too soon,
So the lady in the first-floor back says!

This Song may be Sung in Public without fee or Licence Except at Music Halls.
CATCH 'EM ALIVE OH!
(KETCH 'EM ALIVE OH! NAR THEN WHO WANTS TER MIKE 'IS SWEET'ART A PRESENT?)
H.G. BANKS LITH
THESE GENTLEMEN WELCOME THE FLY-PAPERS
Written & Composed by
ARTHUR SELDON
NOW GENTLEMEN YOU MUST ADMIT MY ARGUMENTS ARE UNANSWERABLE
Sung By
GUS ELEN.
Copyright.
LONDON,
HOWARD & Co. 25 Gt MARLBOROUGH St W.
Price 4/-
H.G. BANKS Lith

CATCH 'EM ALIVE OH!

Written & Composed by ARTHUR SELDON.

I aint made Still when it's nine - ty in the shade I
does a bit yer know 'Tis then them wi - ly
flies pre - pare Ter buzz a - round and make folks swear, So
up and down each street I tear A sing - ing as I go

CHORUS.
Catch em a - live oh, catch em a - live oh!... If they once get on ther
Repeat ff
gum... they'll soon be in kingdom come Catch em a - live oh, catch em a -
- live oh!... I'm a bout the Fly - est man a - bout the town.
1º
2º
town........

CATCH EM ALIVE OH!

1

To sell fly-papers is my trade
A fortchin at it, I aint made
Still when it's 90 in ther shade
I does a bit yer know
'Tis then them wily flies prepare
Ter buzz around and make folks swear
So up and down each street I tear
A singin as I go.

CHORUS.
Catch em alive oh! catch em alive oh!
If they once get on ther gum they'll pop off ter kingdom come
Catch em alive oh! catch em alive oh!
Oh! I am ther flyest man about ther town.

2

Two sheets a penny that's ther price
They'll make a home a paradise
As orniments they're also nice
They're used by ther a-leet (elite)
Bald-headed toffs they looks on me
As they're best friend and jumps wiv glee
When in ther distance they can see
Me, coming down ther street. (wiv my chorus)

CHORUS. Catch em alive oh! &c.

3

The Grand Old Man last week met me
I'll buy yer stock right out sèz 'e
He did so, now sez I may-be
You'll tell me what they're for
Said 'e, ther fact is I pro-pose
Wiv these ter gag my Tory foes
I'll stick em on their mouths, so as
They cant speak anymore

CHORUS.
Yes! I'll gag em alive oh, gag em alive oh!
It's a dirty trick but still, I must pass that 'ome rule Bill
And gag em alive oh, gag em alive oh!
For I am the flyest member in ther house!

EXTRA VERSE.

Some people fink that flies is dence
Devoid of all hintelligence
That only shows yer want of sense
If you fink flies cant talk
They knows as much as you an' me
I've studied them and know yer see
They're lingo's 'ard ter learn may be
It's like learning 'ow ter walk.

Patter. Just like a bloomin kid learning 'ow ter walk, you should watch em as I do, why only last week I saw a whole family of flies, Father, Mother, Sisters, Aunt, and all settle on a copy of the "Echo" which contained a full copy of Mr. Dillon's speech. They only started like this, (Buzz-er-er-er) I knew what he was saying, I'm a bit of a liar myself, but I cant stand this and then drop'd dead and all ther family flew to ther nearest ink pot and drowned themselves. There's Ink-telligence; before I go does anybody want ter buy their sweetheart a nice present? yer dont, Then I must go down the next street, shouting

CHORUS. Catch em alive oh! &c.

This Song may be Sung in Public without fee or Licence, Except at Music Halls.

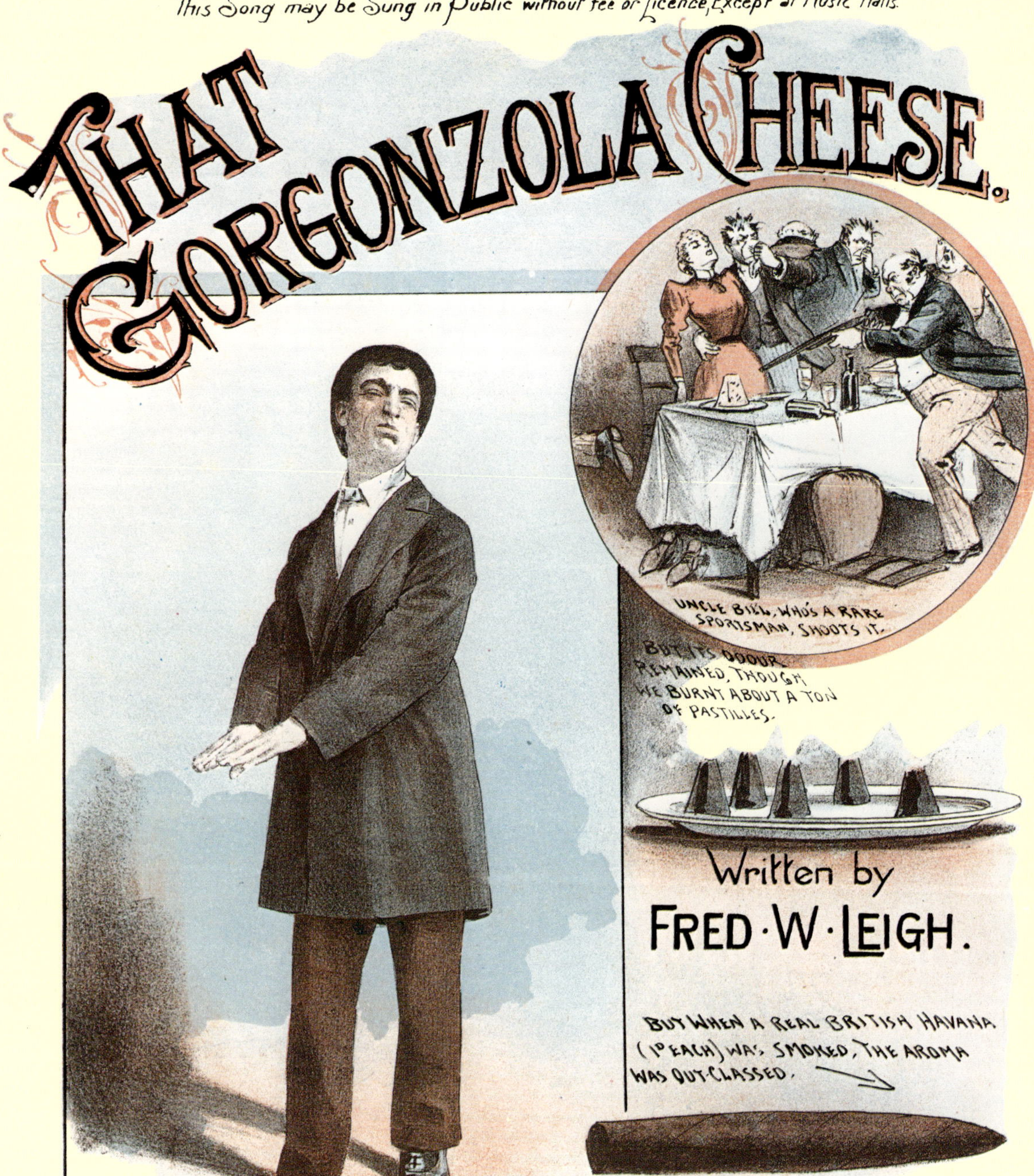

Composed and Sung By

HARRY CHAMPION.

LONDON, HOWARD & Co. 25, Gt. MARLBOROUGH St. W

Price 4/-

NEW YORK SPAULDING & GRAY 16, WEST 27TH St.

OH! THAT GORGONZOLA CHEESE.

WRITTEN BY FRED. W. LEIGH. COMPOSED & SUNG BY HARRY CHAMPION.

ARRANGED BY JOHN S. BAKER.

p
My wife late_ly bought a Gor_gon_zo_la cheese, She saw it in a shop marked
"cheap;"
She thought that her lov_ing husband it would please, If
on_ly till my birth_day it would keep.
She placed that cheese
safe_ly in a drawer, A month went by or per_haps a lit_tle more; Some

friends came on my birthday and the dinner went off great, But when the missus put the Gor_gon

_zo_la on a plate.

CHORUS.

Oh! that Gor_gon_zo_la cheese!

1st time *p*, 2nd *ff*.

sfz

Must have been un_health_y I sup_pose, For the old Tom-cat fell a

corpse up_on the mat, When the "niff" got up its nose;--------------

Talk about the flavour of the crackling on the pork, Nothing could have been so
strong, As the beau_ti_ful ef flu_vi_a that filled our house, When the
Gor_gon_zo_la cheese went wrong.
1st time.
2nd time.
wrong.
ff

My wife lately bought a Gorgonzola cheese;
She saw it in a shop marked "cheap."
You see, she thought her loving husband it would please,
If only till my birthday it would keep.
She locked that cheese up safely in a drawer;
A month passed by, or, perhaps a little more,
Some friends came on my birthday, and the dinner went off "great;"
At last, the missus put the Gorgonzola on a plate.

Oh! that Gorgonzola cheese,
It wasn't over healthy, I suppose;
For our Tom-cat fell a corpse upon the mat,
When the "niff" got up his nose.
Talk about the flavour of the "crackling on the pork!"
Nothing could have been so strong,
As the beautiful effluvia that filled our house
When the Gorgonzola cheese went wrong.

My wife felt a bit offended just *becos*
The company exclaimed, "Great Scott!"
Declared they'd like to know what animal it was,
And asked me if a license I had got.
The fire went dead clean out, and so did one
Of my old pals, who came back with a gun.
Said he, "Look out! I'm going to fire; that cheese I mean to kill."
But when he'd smashed it all to bits, it got more lively still.

(CHORUS.)

When those bits had done a waltz about the place,
At "touch" they soon began to play.
But when two pieces down the passage had a race,
I thought I'd got the hydrophobi-a.
We burned pastilles, but, lor! they did no good.
Destroy that cheese we thought we never should.
But when someone began to puff a good old "penny smoke,"
The Gorgonzola cried, "I'm done! it's time for me to croak.

(CHORUS.)

SLIGHT MISTAKE ON THE PART OF MY VALET.

LONDON: Copyright. Price 4/=
HOWARD AND C° Music Publishers and Printers, 25 GREAT MARLBOROUGH S^t^ W.
NEW · YORK: SPAULDING & GRAY, 16 WEST 27th St.

H. G. BANKS. Lith.

A SLIGHT MISTAKE ON THE PART OF MY VALET.

WRITTEN BY BENNETT SCOTT. COMPOSED BY A. J. MILLS.

ARRANGED BY JOHN S. BAKER.

My va - let is a stu - pid ass, he
is, u - pon my word, As
I leave ev' - ry - thing to him, mis -
takes he makes ab - surd; Last
p

night there was a fan - cy ball, I

said to James "Now please At -

tire me as a Ca - va - lier, he

bunged me in - to these.

CHORUS.
Slight mis - take, Slight mis - take; The
mf
dan - cers took me for an old Aunt Sal - ly; As
rall.
a tempo.
soon as I made my de - but, The girls had fits and simply through, Slight mis -
take on the part of my va - let
ff
D.C.

My valet is a stupid ass, he is, upon my word,
As I leave everything to him mistakes he makes absurd:
Last night there was a fancy ball, I said to James, "Now please
Attire me as a cavalier _ he bunged me into these _
Slight mistake _ Slight mistake _
The dancers took me for an old Aunt Sally,
As soon as I made my bebut the girls had fits and simply through
Slight mistake on the part of my valet.

One evening I played baccarat with Lord de Coffee Grounds.
His Lordship lost a small amount, about a thousand pounds.
Then said I'm stoney broke, old boy, can you lend me two d?"
I sent the valet out to change a threepenny bit for me.
Slight mistake _ Slight mistake _
I told him to be quick and not to dally,
I wanted coppers _ I did grin _ he brought some big fat plicemen in,
Slight mistake on the part of my valet.

I'm very fond of pastry _ er _ you know the sort I mean,
The puffy, not the duffy kind _ with jam stuck in between,
One evening feeling peckish to that stupid chap I said,
"Go forth and fetch some pastry" but the silly josser made _
Slight mistake _ Slight mistake _
He's barmy on the ladies of the ballet,
I wanted tarts, it made me swear, he brought some girls with auburn hair,
Slight mistake on the part of my valet.

I stayed once at a big hotel, and said to James, my man,
Just fetch the number of my room as quickly as you can;
Somehow he made a bloomer for that night I do declare,
I wandered in the rooms used by a newly married pair.
Slight mistake _ Slight mistake _
You bet I felt a little bit tral-lalli,
Said I, "Excuse me if I'm rude, I hope and trust I don't intrude,
Slight mistake on the part of my valet."

EXTRA VERSE.

While staying with my friend the Duke down at his place in Kent,
I met some doosed fine girls and a jolly time I spent,
When I was leaving someone dropped my trunk _ the silly lout,
And all the Duke's best forks and spoons and silver plate fell out.
Slight mistake _ Slight mistake _
The way the Duke addressed me wasn't pally,
You've got my electro plate said he _ What! ain't they silver? gracious me _
Slight mistake on the part of my valet.

This Song must not be Sung in Music Halls or Theatres without Permission.

THE "BOBBIES" OF THE QUEEN.

WHO IS IT ON NIGHT DUTY SMOKES A PIPE OR HAS A DOZE?

WHO IS IT THINKS THAT TELLING LIES IS SUCH AN AWFUL SIN.

CHORUS.

Bold Policemen — keep the peace men,
Oh! don't the cookies love us — they think no men above us,
We take the Cake and Biscuit too when we come on the Scene,
Not the Soldiers nor the Sailors but the "Bobbies" of the Queen.

KIM ON, YE UNMUZZLED WAGABONE.

WHO ARE GREAT AT RUNNING POOR UNMUZZLED BOW-WOWS IN?

HULLO! — WHO THE — WHAT THE — WHERE ARE THEY? —

WHO SEES THAT ALL THE PRETTY GIRLS GET SAFELY O'ER THE STREET?

WHO IS IT APPEARS WHEN THE ROW'S ALL OVER.

Written by
EARDLEY TURNER,
Composed by
MISS MAUD SANTLEY,

Sung by
MISS MAUD SANTLEY.

Price 4/-

LONDON;
HOWARD & Co Music Publishers and Printers, 25 Gt. MARLBOROUGH St. W
NEW YORK: W. B. GRAY & Co 76 West 27th St

H. G. BANKS, Lith.

THE "BOBBIES" OF THE QUEEN.

WRITTEN BY
EARDLEY TURNER.

COMPOSED BY
MAUD SANTLEY.

You've sung a_bout the Na_vy and our brave and bold Jack Tars, You've
sung of Tom_my At_kins and our gal_lant sons of Mars; But
what a_bout the "boys in blue" who prom_e_nade the street They're
wor_thy of a song of praise, for who is there can beat_
p

CHORUS.
Bold po - lice - men keep the peace, men Oh, don't the cookies love us they
a tempo.
think no men a - bove us, We take the cake and bis - cuit too, when
rallo
col canto.
we come on the scene, Not the sol - diers, nor the sai - lors, but the
"Bob - bies" of the Queen.
f
8va

THE "BOBBIES" OF THE QUEEN.

WRITTEN BY
EARDLEY TURNER.

COMPOSED BY
MAUD SANTLEY.

2

Who is it guards you every day from all our country's foes?
Who is it on night duty smokes a pipe or has a doze?
Who is it thinks that telling lies is such an awful sin?
And who are great at running poor unmuzzled bow-wows in?
Bold Policemen, &c.

3

Who sees that all the pretty girls get safely o'er the street?
Who is it holds you gently up when overcome by—heat?
And who are they when rows are on and shrieking fills the air,
Who—just an hour afterwards—are certain to be there?
Bold Policemen, &c.

London: HOWARD & Co., 25, Great Marlborough St., W.

NEW YORK: W. B. GRAY & Co., 16, WEST 27TH STREET.

(H & Co. 3181.)

This Song may be sung anywhere without Fee or License.
ON THE DAY KING EDWARD GETS HIS CROWN ON.
CHORUS.
Up and down the Strand, Up and down the Strand,
Wait until you hear the trumpets sound,
Shouting Hip, Hurray, all the blooming day,
When our good King Edward's Crowned.
Written and Composed by
MARK LORNE AND HARRY PLEON,
Sung by
HARRY PLEON.
AUNTIE'S GOING TO HAVE A BATH.
FATHER'S GOING TO GIVE A DINNER, & HE'LL EAT THE LOT HIMSELF.
Copyright.
Price 4/-
HOPWOOD & CREW LTD
LATE HOWARD & Co
Music Publishers and Printers.
25, GREAT MARLBOROUGH St LONDON. W.

ON THE DAY KING EDWARD GETS HIS CROWN ON.

WRITTEN AND COMPOSED BY MARK LORNE AND HARRY PLEON.

There's a good time com-ing soon for the fam-i-ly, On the
day King Ed-ward gets his crown on. Pa-
rad-ing up and down the Strand, all of us you'll see, On the
day King Ed-ward gets his crown on. We'll

all buy pen - ny tick - lers, and won't we have a lark?
All the p'lice-men mo - ther meets she'll cud - dle in the dark;
Fa - ther's going to smack 'em on their vac - ci - na - tion mark, On the
day King Ed - ward gets his crown on.

CHORUS.
Up and down the Strand–
Up and down the Strand–
f
Wait un-til you hear the trumpets sound.
Shouting Hip Hurray!
Cres:
All the bloom-ing day When our good King Edward's crowned.
f
D.C.

Encore Verses.

They're going to do a lot of things to help both you and me
On the day King Edward gets his crown on.
Banish all the Pro-Boers from this country
On the day King Edward gets his crown on.
Now I've heard on good authority, so I'll put it plain,
That a certain well-known General dismissed will not remain,
For they'll reinstate old Buller to his old command again,
On the day King Edward gets his crown on.

Oh, the decorations on our house will be one of the sights
On the day King Edward gets his crown on.
We'll have candles wrapped in paper, perhaps incandescent lights,
On the day King Edward gets his crown on.
For a banner hang out father's shirt tied with coloured rag,
We've no gun to fire a royal salute, so we'll bust a paper-bag,
And change the baby's bottle for a windmill or a flag,
On the day King Edward gets his crown on.

We've already saved up threepence for that glorious event,
On the day King Edward gets his crown on.
And if father backs a winner, we'll pay sixpence off the rent,
On the day King Edward gets his crown on.
We'll all go in for luxuries-never mind the bills,
Have Woodbines, whelks, and other game, don't care if it kills,
And we've promised to buy grandma a box of Beecham's Pills,
On the day King Edward gets his crown on.

ON THE DAY KING EDWARD GETS HIS CROWN ON.

By MARK LORNE and HARRY PLEON.

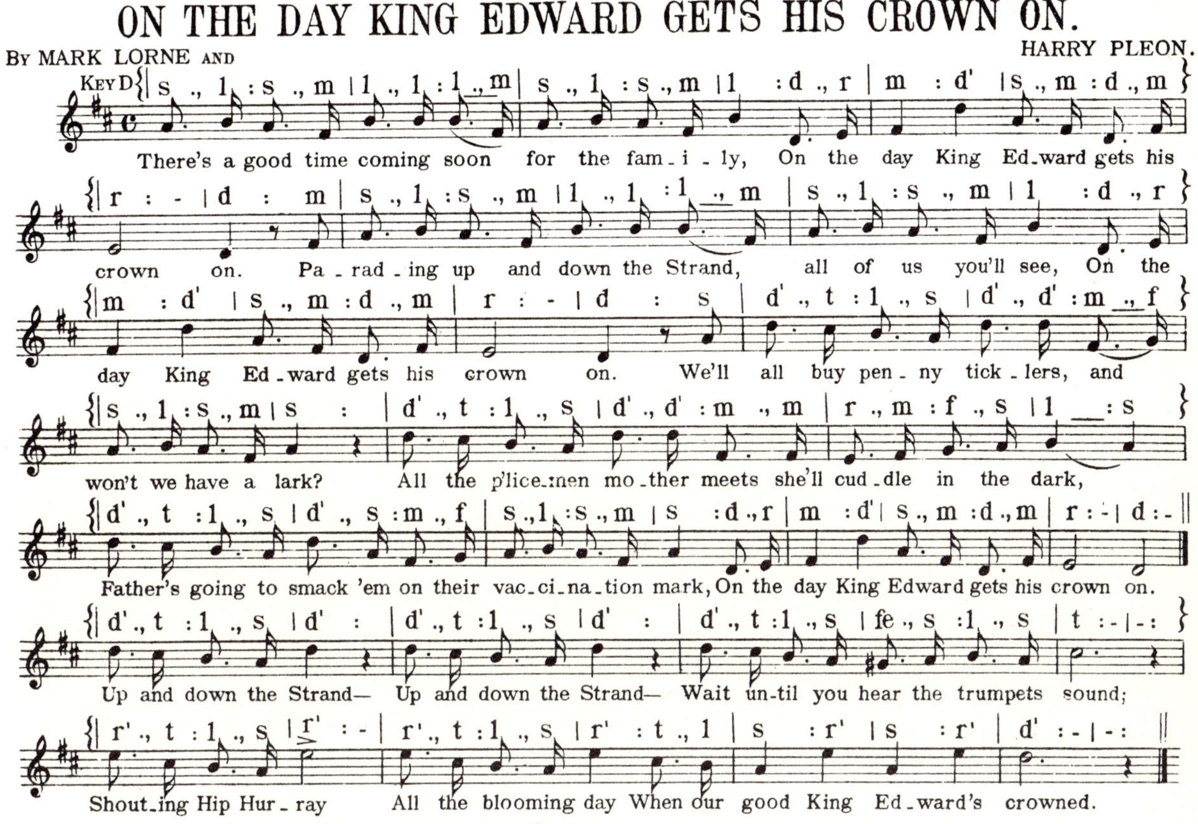

2

Father's going to change his socks and Auntie have a bath,
On the day King Edward gets his crown on.
With a brick we'll hit the landlord to make the baby laugh,
On the day King Edward gets his crown on.
The lodger's going to get blind drunk, as soon as day begins,
Sister's wearing bloomers fixed up with safety-pins,
To celebrate the great event mother will have twins,
On the day King Edward gets his crown on.

3

The hens are going to lay fried eggs, already to be taken,
On the day King Edward gets his crown on.
Our old cock is going to try to lay a rasher of bacon,
On the day King Edward gets his crown on.
We'll unchain the Gorgonzola, kill the neighbours all for miles,
Should the tax-collector call, Towzer will be all smiles,
And the tom-cat's made his mind up to go on the tiles,
On the day King Edward gets his crown on.

4

Father's going to give a dinner to prove he's lots of pelf,
On the day King Edward gets his crown on.
To make the neighbours jealous he'll eat it all himself,
On the day King Edward gets his crown on.
Auntie'll be dress'd in kakhi, ribbons all down her back,
We can't afford to buy new clothes, but in loyalty will not lack,
Ma's going to patch up father's pants with a piece of Union Jack,
On the day King Edward gets his crown on.

HOPWOOD & CREW, Ltd. (Late Howard & Co.)
25, Great Marlborough Street, London. W.

New York: W. B. Gray & Co., 16, West 27th. Street.

This Song must not be sung in Music Halls and Theatres, without permission.

AN OLD MAN'S DARLING.

Written and Composed by

FRED MURRAY,

and

GEORGE EVERARD.

CHORUS

Some girls, when they think of marriage, get about all they can.
Some girls, when they think of marriage, fancy a nice young man.
But I'm not so inclined, for none of those things I crave;
I'd rather be an old man's darling, than a young man's slave

Sung by

MISS VESTA VICTORIA.

HOPWOOD & CREW LTD

Late HOWARD & Co Music Publishers and Printers.

Price 2/- net.

25, GREAT MARLBOROUGH STREET, LONDON, W.

NEW YORK: W. B. GRAY & Co 16, West 27th Street

AN OLD MAN'S DARLING.

Written and Composed by FRED MURRAY & GEORGE EVERARD.

Some girls, soon as ev - er they get in their teens,
Al - ways turn their minds to love.
They im - ag - ine that a young man's best, But
take my word, I've put 'em to the test.

I've dis - covered that an old man's bet - ter, When

all is said and done, Though his

hair may be grey, in his sweet old way, He can

Rall:

make your life a hap - py one.

Rall:

CHORUS.
Some girls, when they think of mar-riage, get a-bout all they can,
Some girls, when they think of mar-riage, fan-cy a nice young man;
But I'm not so in-clined, for none of these things I crave, I'd
rather be an old man's dar-ling than a young man's slave. slave.
1
2
ff
D.C.

AN OLD MAN'S DARLING.

WRITTEN AND COMPOSED BY FRED MURRAY & GEORGE EVERARD.

2

Young men, soon as ever they take on a wife,
Start their antics right away.
All the day he'll lay about in bed;
The wife must find the butter and the bread.
What a difference with a dear old fellow!
He is all that's true and good.
No "wire" do you get, "I'm detained, my pet".
No! he comes home as a husband should. (CHORUS.)

3

Old chaps, when they take a wife and settle down,
Settle down in real good style.
They're not jealous like the young men, no!
For they will trust you anywhere you go.
Ladies, take this good advice I'm giving,
As this life you go through,
Be it pleasure or strife, his one thought's his wife,
He's a husband and a father, too. (CHORUS.)

HOPWOOD & CREW, LTD: (LATE HOWARD & CO.)
25, Great Marlborough Street, London. W.
NEW YORK: W. B. GRAY & CO., 16, WEST 27TH STREET.

H & C. Ltd. 3512.

4. INTERVAL!

Bacon & Greens – Published 14 February 1859
Sam Cowell was one of the earliest stars in the music hall firmament: born in 1820, he made his début on the British stage on 1 July 1840 and his meteoric rise to fame brought widespread public recognition, high financial rewards and a certain security which allowed him to marry in 1842. Graduating via the Cyder Cellars, the Cole Hole and Evans (late Joys), he was brought to the 'Canterbury' by Charles Morton – earning up to £80 per week.

His most noted songs were 'Villikins and his Dinah', which he borrowed from Frederick Robson (another well-known music hall artiste), and 'The Railway Porter' – written in conjunction with Charles Sloman.

Touring many times on the Morton circuit, he was one of the first British music hall artistes to be 'exported' to America where he was greatly acclaimed in 1864. On this particular tour, however, he contracted an illness which, on returning to England, was aggravated by his heavy drinking and ultimately resulted in his tragically early death at the age of forty-four later in that year.

'Bacon & Greens' is one of the typical 'food' ballads prevalent at that time – a hybrid song of pop and folk idiom with a pleasant enough melody – note the additional verse which was used as an obligatory encore in place of a 'moral'.

Hop Light Loo – Published circa 1860
Professionally classed as a 'Negro Delineator', E. W. Mackney was in the van of the black-faced singers to appear on the British halls. Born in 1825, he played at Evans (late Joys) in his early career singing on the same nights as Sam Cowell. From there he progressed to become another artiste in the Charles Morton stable – probably arriving at the 'Canterbury' at the same time as Sam Cowell. He was at once billed as 'The Great Mackney' and this led to the celebrated skirmish between himself and Morton:

'I wish you wouldn't do that,' he protested, 'it makes me feel such a terrible sense of responsibility' – to which Morton replied, 'You be hanged! I pay you a salary and all you are concerned with is doing your business to the best of your ability. It is my business to bill you in what I think is the best audience-attracting manner.'

His most celebrated song was 'The whole hog or none' which he continued to sing on the 'boards' for most of his long life – he died in 1909.

The cover of 'Hop Light Loo' bears a stylish portrayal of Mackney caught up in the excitement of his act. The artist R. J. Hamerton (1809–1905) was famous for this type of vignette and started as a humorous sketcher contributing to many magazines and periodicals including *Punch*. The song itself, although never registered at Stationers' Hall, was probably published in 1860 at the height of Mackney's 'Canterbury' days. (It is necessary to remark here that the Hopwood & Crew stock numbers in the early 1860s were often out of chronological sequence.) The ballad was written especially for Mackney by G. W. Hunt (1839–1904) and is one of the earliest works of this prodigious songwriter. The melody heralds the coming popularity and zest of the minstrel troups – one can almost hear an accompaniment of a jangling banjo – while the lyrics present a multi-racial situation brought about by the new freedom under the banishment of slavery in Great Britain (and in America a few years later following the American Civil War). In those days, a negro on the streets of London or elsewhere in the British Isles was still a rarity and the idea of a mixed marriage conjured nothing more in the mind of the populace than a spectacle at a 'freak show' and a curious novelty to be stared at and smiled upon.

Polly Perkins of Paddington Green – Published 22 June 1863
From the salon circuit to the 'Canterbury' Harry Clifton (1824–1872) was adored and applauded. He sang in provincial halls and theatres as well as at soirées and masonics. Most of his songs had a strong moralistic theme which pleased the 'Upper Ten' and 'uplifted' the 'Lower Five'. He toured with his own concert party whose leading lady, Fanny Edwards, he later married – in her own right she was a minor music hall star.

Clifton wrote over 500 ballads – borrowing tunes from various sources including Charles Coote, Jr and J. Tinney (a popular dance tune composer): his better known ditties include 'Shelling green peas', 'On board the Kangaroo', 'The weeping willer', 'Dark girl dressed in blue', 'Pulling hard against the stream', 'Rocky road to Dublin' and 'The Calico printer's clerk'.

'Polly Perkins of Paddington Green' has survived in community repertoires for over a hundred years and represents one of the few ballads that Clifton wrote without a moralistic theme. The lovelorn expression of the broken-hearted milkman thrown aside in favour of a bow-legged bus conductor has been cleverly depicted by a cover artist who sadly remains unidentified, yet whose style immediately suggests Concanen. The tune is based upon a very old folk melody which appears as 'Nightingales sing' in many folk song collections. It was further borrowed via Clifton's 'Polly Perkins' by the Tyneside composer George Ridley as a vehicle for his lyrics to the immortal 'love' song 'Cushie Butterfield'. There have been many disputes as to which version came first but on the dates alone this chicken and egg teaser comes down firmly on the side of Clifton.

Ticket of Leave Man – Published circa 1864
Alfred Peck Stevens was born in London in 1839. He worked for a while in a solicitor's office in Lincoln's Inn but the lure of the theatre made him give up his career for the 'boards' as an actor and a one-man entertainer and thence as a music hall artiste under the name of 'Alfred Vance'. His first appearance was in 1864 and he achieved success as a female impersonator and a character actor in the guise of 'Algie Dashon' – the heavy swell. His most popular songs included 'Heavy swell' and 'Act on the square'. It was at the Sun, Knightsbridge on Boxing Day 1888 that Vance literally made his last appearance: he was suffering from nervous exhaustion and fell dead on stage after delivering the last words of his song 'Not guilty'. The audience thought that it was all part of his act and applauded vigorously - such were the strains upon a music hall artiste to give his all for his audience.

Again we have no clear knowledge of the exact publication date of 'Ticket of leave man' but Vance advertised in the trade papers that he was to perform it in October 1864. The song was based upon a character from the plot of a play produced in 1863 bearing the same title: a convict is allowed home by 'ticket of leave' from Australia and takes up with his old ways and compatriots in somewhat similar surroundings to those of Dickens' 'Artful Dodger'. The lyric of the song is written as though the character were of Eastern European extraction (there were many such immigrants in East London in those days) and the whole characterization is reminiscent of Fagin.

Slap Bang Here We Are Again – Published circa 1865
This merry drinking song was performed by Vance in his 'swell' characterization. Unfortunately there is no note of a Stationers' Hall entry, yet Charles Sheard published a polka version late in 1865 – therefore one can deduce that the original song, being so popular, warranted other publishers such as Sheard quickly issuing various salon piano versions. The song became so popular that indeed a multitude of versions were printed – the chorus setting the right jovial atmosphere for any self-respecting music hall and which may still be heard from time to time today – so infectious is its melody.

Up in a Balloon – Published 21 May 1868
George Leybourne was born at Gateshead in 1842 and worked as a labourer at a marine engineer's in Westminster Bridge Road. The London music hall scene soon attracted him and he obtained his first break at Gilbert's music hall, Whitechapel using the name of Joe Saunders so as not to embarrass his family by associating with a trade that was still frowned upon. He was tall and good-looking, had a magnetic personality and this, coupled with a fine baritone singing voice soon brought him fame. Chairman J. J. Poole invented the phrase 'Lion Comique' in his honour and such was his success that he reverted to using his own name and became the most highly paid artiste of the time – earning from £30 a week in 1867 to more than £100 a week when he died in 1884. The money he earned was generously spent on audiences and friends alike and his reliance on drink, especially champagne, facilitated by his high income and his endeavour to maintain his 'swell' image, took its toll and eventually killed him. He set the pace for the other Lion Comiques, defiantly campaigning via the medium of the halls on national issues which invariably upset and annoyed the Establishment – yet because of his popularity, neither the Lord Chamberlain nor the authorities dared silence him. It was also true to say that the young 'bucks' of the Establishment classes looked up to him for a lead.

His most famous songs besides 'Up in a balloon' were 'The daring young man on the flying trapeze' and 'Champagne Charlie'. The beautiful melodic line of 'Up in a balloon' was one of G. W. Hunt's earlier successes at a time when he was turning out songs for many artistes with the regularity of a machine: topicality was an important element in most music hall songs of this period and ballooning had become the craze. The young Nelly Power introduced the female version of this song (published on 2 October 1868), the lyrics of which were written by her mother. It may be of some interest to note that it was nine years later that G. W. Hunt's 'War Song' earned him the name 'Jingo', when one reads the penultimate line of the song.

The cover artist, Henry Maguire represented the youngest of three generations in a family of fine art students. He was a prolific illustrator and preferred straight portraiture based on photographs: he worked with Concanen for a time but lacked Concanen's distinctive sharpness.

Fashionable Fred – Published circa 1868
It can be said that Walter Laburnum (real name Joe Davis) was the poor man's George Leybourne. Born in 1847, he was considered a 'Minor Lion' and bore a strong resemblance to Leybourne and who sent up Leybourne's gimmick of riding in a carriage and four, by driving between halls in a donkey cart and four 'tigers' wearing shoe-black hats. Laburnum was a master of cockney rhyming slang (probably an art acquired from the time he had operated as a bookie) – his billing read 'Walter Laburnum – The Longest Living Lath of Laughter'.

In 'Fashionable Fred' we can view Laburnum at his celebrated pastime of 'lathing' Leybourne – a 'swell' song with a pleasant strolling tune to which he could swagger nonchalantly around the stage and which any 'dirty urchin' would be content to whistle.

Brown the Tragedian – Published 1870
Arthur Lloyd was born in 1839 into a family of Scottish music hall fame – his father was a well-loved performer in the Scottish halls. Arthur himself first appeared in London in 1862 and was soon a favourite with the 'Pavillion' audiences; with his good baritone voice, he could carry off character sketches and his biggest success in his lifetime was 'Immensikoff' although other songs that he originated such as 'Not for Joseph' and 'Married to a mermaid' have fared better over the years. In style he was the last survivor of the Lion Comique generation and he even billed himself right up to his demise in 1904 as 'the last Lion Comique'.

The cover of 'Brown the Tragedian' was designed by Richard Childs – an artist who experimented with pictorial calligraphy and whose output in the 1860s and 70s was nothing but prolific. However, the life-style of the music hall artiste seems to have impinged upon his character for like many a music hall artiste, his dependence on alcohol eventually ended his career.

The song has an exquisite text including a lyrical patter that would attract the attentions of any Micawber. Although it is not quite in the same vein as 'The night I appeared as Macbeth' there are clear resonances set up by this history of trials and tribulations of an actor – maybe even of some music hall hopefuls!

The Rustic Damsel – Published 23 February 1871
Harry Liston first trod the 'boards' in his late teens and established a name for himself touring in the north of England as a dialect comedian. At the instigation of J. J. Poole in 1865, when Liston was twenty-two, he made his London début at 'the Met'. In the following year he toured the halls as a member of Arthur Lloyd's concert party eventually founding his own little company. Music hall audiences warmed to his characterizations – his travelling Jewish glazier – his Dutchman – his wizened old man. The two songs which have stayed the course of time are 'Nobody's child' and 'When Johnny comes marching home'. He continued with his concerts like 'Merry moments'

throughout his life – untypically long for a music hall artiste – he died in 1929.

'The rustic damsel' is a strange mixture of bowdlerized folk tune and Villikinesque lyrics. The tune was probably from the same roots as that used for 'The daring young man on the flying trapeze' and that used twenty years later for Percy French's 'The mountains of Mourne' – indeed the melody has many folk variants stretching far back into the eighteenth century. The lyrics are a combination of Cockney eloquence and phrase spoonerisms effecting charm out of what would otherwise be a tale of gruesome tragedy. The song was originally published by M. Gunn & Son, 61 Grafton Street, Dublin and was later purchased sometime in the 1880s by J. Blockley.

Captain Cuff – Published 31 March 1877
Following on his successes such as 'Gold, Gold, Gold!', and the threshold of his great 'Macdermott's War Song', G. W. Hunt presented Leybourne with this ditty of a 'masher' who maintains his finery despite poverty. There is a story that Hunt and Leybourne lived at one time in the same house where Hunt would play the piano downstairs while Leybourne rested upstairs: whenever Hunt, extemporizing on the piano, hit upon a good tune, Leybourne would call out his approval. In the case of this song, however, it seems likely that Leybourne must have had his mind elsewhere when calling out to Hunt for the song is saved only by its 'telling' lyrics (and whatever happened to the third verse is a mystery that only the compositor or maybe the Lord Chamberlain could have unravelled). The cover drawing is a superb example of Alfred Bryan's skill in extracting the charisma and panache of an artiste and transferring these intangibles successfully, and with no less vitality, on to paper.

Dear Old Pals – Published 23 July 1877
Born in 1845, Michael John Farrell's first job of work was that of a seaman, but he left the sea to tour fairgrounds and, using the name Gilbert Hastings Farrell, he completed his apprenticeship and switched to music hall. He started his new career singing at the Grecian Saloon, City Road soon after changing his name yet again to G. H. Macdermott: he even tried straight acting for a time and was responsible for the stage version of Dickens' *The Mystery of Edwin Drood*, yet music hall for him was always his mistress and his first success came when he sang 'The Scamp' in 1873 which somewhat scandalized the audiences by the use of the word 'damn' in the lyrics, and accordingly he became a name on every theatre-goer's lips – this marked the turning point in his career, and, following the upsurge of the 'heavy swell' image portrayed by Vance and Leybourne, Macdermott decided to modify this image till it fitted him like a glove. Although he did not possess the voice of Leybourne, he attracted audiences by his comments on current affairs and the English political scene, and he became the foremost Lion Comique in this field. At the height of his fame he could demand £100 minimum per week, yet his outspokeness ruffled the feathers of the Lord Chamberlain's office on many occasions and he was finally banned from appearing in any West End theatre in the late 1880s. However, Macdermott had learnt a few tricks himself from observing the political processes in Parliament over the years, and he neatly side-stepped the issue by retiring as an artiste and re-appearing as manager of various music halls including The Forresters, Mile End Road. He married twice in his life – the

second time to Annie Milburn, herself a music hall artiste and daughter of an old stager, Gem Milburn. Macdermott died of cancer on 8 May 1901 at his Clapham home and with his death came the end of an era – that of the Lion Comique.

'Dear old pals' was a Hunt song which followed closely on the great success of 'Macdermott's War Song' but it is only remembered today for its chorus. It was premiered at the Royal Cambridge Music Hall on 22 June 1877 at a benefit night for Fred Albert – the *Entr'acte* remarked, 'A first rate convivial lay about "Dear Old Pals" by Mr. G. W. Hunt which is likely to be much in request' – an underrated statement indeed for a song which rates second only to 'Nellie Dean' in pub repertoires.

For some reason it took a month before the song was published – perhaps its popularity took everybody by surprise, although at 2d per copy royalty, G. W. Hunt must have been surprised all the way to the bank.

Little Miss Muffet sat on a Tuffet – Published 1 August 1879
The exquisite Concanen cover is enough to sell this song to anyone without an ear for music, but the song has a charm of its own (complete with hidden undertones) which fully rates Concanen's embellishment. The chorus is virtually all of the well-known nursery rhyme except for the last line which provides a subtle twist to any straightforward meaning presented in the preceding four lines. It is amusing to note that propriety was satisfied by the marriage of the two characters in the last verse – fulfilling Victorian moral justice and at the same time confirming the suspicions of double meaning in the preceding part of the song.

Although the cover states that this song was printed on 22 July, this was purely for Stationers' Hall registration – the official publication date was in fact ten days later.

Tuner's Oppor-Tuner-Ty – Published 15 November 1879
According to the *Entr'acte*, Fred Coyne was 'a very talented comic vocalist, and will, we fancy, in the course of time hold a leading position among our star artistes'. Although Coyne never achieved the dizzy heights of the main Lion Comiques, he nevertheless remained a firm favourite with audiences for many decades with his comic ballads.

'Tuner's Oppor-Tuner-Ty' was written by Fred Coyne and Harry Adams and assigned to Howard & Co on 29 January 1879 with another song for £12. The lyric overflows with double entendres and follows the well-laid pattern prevalent in folk songs such as 'The German Clock Mender (-Winder)' and 'The Coachman' whereby the trade and its associated tools are synonymous with sexual meanings – e.g. 'to keep her piano in tune', 'fingering the keys' and 'he tuned whene'er he got the opportunity'. The domestic confrontation with the husband is aptly illustrated by Concanen using his adroit skill – note the symbolism of the hat on the hall hanger and the barometer reading 'stormy'.

The Bulls Won't Bellow – Published 1880
Sam Torr was born in Nottingham in 1850 and in his early music hall career he styled himself upon Sam Cowell – his first success being the topical song 'The wreck of the North Fleet'. He played many character parts but finally settled into emulating the Lion Comiques. This song, however, dates from the end of

his 'character' portrayal period. Torr tried his hand several times at management but always came back to the 'boards' – he died in 1923. In his portrayal of a broken-hearted agricultural worker (note his costume of a stove-pipe hat and smock in the early H. G. Banks lithograph), he sings of the loss of his sweetheart Jane who has been lured away from the farm by a city swell. It seems that the whole farmyard is suffering along with himself and one can draw a parallel in style between this song with its pleasant melody and poignant lyrics and that of Harry Clifton's 'Polly Perkins'.

In my fust 'Usband's Time – Published 6 January 1882
Born in 1844, Herbert Campbell soon made a name for himself by his size alone – he weighed around nineteen stone. Originally he entered the halls as a black-faced minstrel but he then turned to the role in which the public knew and loved him – a female impersonator and the first pantomime dame. (He was partnered many times by Dan Leno, especially in roles such as the 'Ugly Sisters'.) On an assignment in 1881 he signed himself as 'H. Posthumous Campbell' – whether this was his real name or a passing comical whim, only he knew. He died in 1904 not long after his 'sister'-in-arms, Dan Leno.

'In my fust 'usband's time' is a typical 'dame' song which would stand well in pantomime today just as it did then. One can imagine the idiosyncrasies of an old woman yearning for the 'good old days' from which Campbell would wring out as much pathos as possible – the patter fills out a musical vamp in which he could deploy his 'business' to any extent that he thought necessary to satisfy his audiences. As in all good pantomime songs both the verse and chorus melody were 'catchy' and could be taken up easily by the audience.

From 1881 onwards, Concanen used a date code on his cover drawings – this code is found under his signature and runs as follows:

HA	=	1881
HB	=	1882
HC	=	1883
HD	=	1884
HE	=	1885

In this case, Concanen had drawn the cover supposedly sometime in December of 1881.

Up went the Price – Published 6 March 1882
The composer of this song, George Ware, was born in 1829 and had his first writing success with 'The House that Jack Built' which won him the Sam Cowell Prize. He acted for a while in music hall himself but became entrenched in the 1850s as a music hall agent (in 1868 he advertised as 'Music Hall agent and diamond merchant'). He wrote many songs for his artistes including 'The whole hog or none' for Mackney, and 'Up went the price' was a great success for Macdermott with its ironic lyrics and whistlable chorus. Ware went on to manage such artistes as Marie Lloyd, and because he had been the first in his field, he advertised, and was generally known as 'the Old Reliable'.

Baa Baa Baa – Published 14 April 1882
'Jolly' John Nash (1830–1901) was one of the foremost exponents of the

'laughing' song – hence the nickname 'Jolly'. He started in music hall at the Oxford in 1861 and quickly achieved public recognition, becoming chairman of the Strand Music Hall in 1863: royal recognition followed later and he was one of the first music hall stars to appear before a member of the royal family – in his case, the Prince of Wales. We are still acquainted today with one of the songs which he made famous over a hundred years ago – 'Little brown jug'.

'Baa Baa Baa' is a melodiously witty ballad of a sheep stealer who claims to be stupid to the point of idiocy in order to fool a judge and jury and so escape sentence. Note how this stratagem is used as a double-edged weapon by this 'country cousin' upon his sly lawyer in the last verse.

She does the Fandango all over the Place – Published 21 July 1883
This song was perhaps the most memorable that Henri Clark ever originated. In early life he had been a 'legitimate' actor and a buffo in grand opera, but he turned to the music hall, however, to more fully exploit his creative talent for characterizations which have been compared with those of Dan Leno. These included 'The Waiter', 'The Barber', 'Railway Porter Dan' and his best-loved chorus song impersonation of 'The Mad Butcher'. At one time George Ware managed his career but by 1893, Clark had progressed to become the manager of the 'Met'.

The humorous artistry of 'Jingo' Hunt is at its best in this song – even the patter, reminiscent of Sam Cowell, does not detract from the Clifton-like lyrics and catchy melody line – it is a whole from which not one section can be removed. Undoubtably, Clark, as depicted on the cover, went through all the motions evoked by the lyrics and so transformed a song into a semi-characterization role.

The House that Jerry Built – Published 10 February 1885
James Fawn set out in music hall in 1877 as a 'Nigger' act but proved himself so versatile an actor that he dropped the 'burnt cork' and, sometimes partnered by Arthur Roberts, created a style which heralded a new generation of performers. He was born James Simmons in 1850 – an unconfirmed story relates that his stage name came about through fawn being his favourite colour.Fawn did many cameo performances and his favourite role was that of a policeman which was in constant demand by his audiences owing to its associated ditty '(If you want to know the time) ask a Policeman'. He maintained this in his act for the rest of his music hall career – he died in 1923.

The trials and tribulations of moving into a suburban house in London in the 1880s are well documented in the lyrics and patter of this so aptly punned 'The house that Jerry built'. Suburban London in those days spread no further than a ten-mile radius from Oxford Circus and many of these dwellings still exist despite the Blitz, slum clearances and home improvement schemes – happily the attendant services have greatly improved since then. The chorus melodically has a sauntering rhythm perhaps more often associated with the 'swell' songs, but given the adapted lyrical usage of the nursery rhyme 'The house that Jack built', an audience would readily appreciate, and join in with, the song.

What Cheer Ria – Published 2 April 1885
Born Kathleen Mahoney in 1857, Bessie Bellwood became the first lady singer of cockney songs, arriving at this role by the uncertain route of Irish ballads. Her repartee was renowned throughout the business and she could master, nay, outshout, the rowdiest audience: she once held a five-minute slanging-match with a fifteen stone coal-heaver during her act, from which he retired hurt and demoralized. Her acts of charity to the poor, such as giving away her possessions, taking in laundry, cleaning homes and looking after children were also known to her audiences – perhaps this is why they loved her – as a genuine person.

Her bohemian life eventually wore her down and her 'no nonsense', larger-than-life character could not withstand the toll of the years of strain, and she died at the early age of thirty-nine.

'What Cheer Ria' fitted Bessie Bellwood's character like a glove – the lyrics and patter enforce her masterful and yet flippant stage manner – the minor key of the verse seems to echo the wretchedness of her self-sacrifice while the modulation to the major key in the chorus provides for the brave, cheerful face she donned for her audiences. If she had never sung another song, she would have always been remembered for this – a fitting epitaph for a truly big-hearted artiste.

The Boy in the Gallery – Published 15 May 1885
The all too tragically short career of Nelly Power is, however, surprising when one realizes the effect she had on her audiences, the still-popular songs that she sang and the innovations that she introduced. Ten years before Vesta Tilley became a famous male impersonator, Nelly Power had established this role. In 1868, at the age of fifteen, she was singing the female version of 'Up in a balloon' which firmly installed her as a favourite in the hearts of her audiences. In 1885 George Ware was her manager and wrote this charming little song for her – a song which is still remembered today albeit by its chorus alone. It spelt out the rapport that Nelly established with even the lowliest member of her audiences – the boy in the gallery. George Ware gave his rights in the song to Nelly and she assigned them to Hopwood & Crew on 2 March 1885 for the sum of £5.

When Marie Lloyd first went in front of the footlights, she 'borrowed' this song without Nelly's permission, but as George Ware was both Nelly's and Marie's agent, and as Nelly died aged thirty-four in 1887, no action was taken. It seems a pity, however, that over the years 'The boy in the gallery' has been falsely accredited to Marie Lloyd when such an artiste as Nelly Power has gone unrecognized.

The Funny Things They Do upon the Sly – Published 30 December 1885
G. W. Hunter, billed as 'the Mark Twain of the Music Halls', was probably the last of the Lion Comiques generation. Although in style he emulated the 'Great Ones', his brand of wry humour places him in a small class of artiste who stood astride both the old and new generations of music hall performers.

Concannen's illustration of the song 'The funny things they do upon the sly' highlights the simplistic skill commanded by G. W. Hunter to carry out his stage act – the winking of his right eye and the touching of his nose.

(These stage gestures were often employed by Leybourne and Macdermott to the same effect.) This song, although without a chorus, has a 'pay-off' line, i.e. the title, which no doubt was vociferously taken up by his audiences – the different situations in each verse culminating with the same all-encompassing conclusion. These typical situations from London's social life were commonplace to Hunter's audiences and therefore the more humorous.

Angels without Wings – Published 4 June 1887
Making her first appearance in 1868 at the age of four, Vesta Tilley was truly born and brought up into the music hall tradition. Her father, Harry Ball, was chairman of 'St George's Hall', Nottingham, where she made her début. Vesta arrived in London in 1878 and opened at the Royal, Holborn, billed as the 'Great Little Tilley' and in the following five years took up the role of the 'Man-About-Town' – establishing male impersonation as an art form. Many critics have declared that she understood the character of this role better than the real-life characters themselves, and that she carried it off better than any other artiste, man or woman. The ballads Vesta sang that have endured over the years include 'After the ball' and 'Following in Father's footsteps'. Royalty and public alike admired her and fittingly she was invited to appear in many Royal Command Performances. Vesta married Walter De Frece, the theatre impressario who was later knighted, and settled down to a quiet life in upper-class social circles after making a farewell performance at the London Coliseum in June 1920. She died at the grand old age of eighty-eight in 1952.

Vesta performed 'Angels without wings' in her male impersonator role (although she is shown otherwise attired in the cover cameo). This song depicts women as angels despite all their blemishes and the chorus floats as angelically as the women in the song would have their admirers believe them to behave. The distinction, between what the women really are and what they would wish to appear, is cleverly counterpoised by the verse being in martial 2/4 time and the chorus in blithe waltz rhythm. The impish irony of the lilting chorus comes with the last line 'Like the men, you're angels, when you're not found out'.

It is interesting to observe that H. G. Banks' cover style had matured since 'The bulls won't bellow' seven years previously, and his use of cameo insets here was in the process of taking over the whole cover – a technique which he later consolidated.

Ti! Hi! Tiddelly Hi! – Published 22 October 1887
Some music hall buffs have classified Harry Rickards as a late Lion Comique but although he came late to the scene, finding fame in his role as a military 'masher', his status coincided more with the new generation of artiste than with that of the old. Born 1842 as Benjamin Leete, he performed in the music halls up and down the country and achieved quite a devoted following, but, after speculating in some unsound investments, he went bankrupt and at the turn of the century left for Australia seeking a new life. Here he founded many music halls and eventually died a rich man in 1911.

Joseph Tabrar wrote many famous songs in his life (he could be rated as a latter-day G. W. Hunt). 'Ti! Hi! Tiddelly Hi!' was one of his earlier works and was written before he came to the attention of the general public with songs such as 'Daddy wouldn't buy me a bow-wow'. Perhaps this song describes the way in which Tabrar seized inspiration for his compositions – its catchy but inane chorus seems to sum up the perplexities of his imaginative talent.

Buy me some Almond Rock – Published 17 March 1893
The eldest of a family of nine, Matilda Wood was born on 12 February 1870. Her father was employed as a waiter at the 'Royal Eagle Tavern' where she made her first appearance under the name of 'Bella Del Mere'. In 1885, she changed her name to Marie Lloyd and had immediate success with the song 'The boy in the gallery', 'borrowed' from Nelly Power. As she grew older, Marie evolved a saucy style in her portrayal of an innocent, yet 'knowing' young lady, and, although most of her songs were not as suggestive or blue as the press made out, her pert embellishments – winks, sly smiles etc – could give a lyric a completely different meaning. In 1887 she married Percy Courtney who turned out to be a wastrel and this led to a divorce in 1894 after he had frittered away all her money. Despite the setback of bringing up a young child, Marie Jr, Marie threw herself into her music hall act more and more touring the British mainland and France, and swiftly became the 'Queen of Hearts' to all her audiences. Love came again in the late 1890s in the person of Alec Hurley, a coster singer, who was popular in the halls. After a long 'attachment' they married in 1907 but by this time Marie far outshone Hurley in the music hall – in fact she was the best-known artiste on four continents! Because of her superstar status and her constant public demand, Hurley faded into the background and in 1913 died of drink, double pneumonia and a broken heart. In the meantime Marie had taken up with Bernard Dillon, a jockey, whom she first met in 1907, and this relationship caused a scandal not only in the British Isles but on a disastrous tour of America, where she was hounded by the self-righteous authorities.

Marie married Dillon in February 1914 but any hope of lasting happiness faded when rows between them, especially when Dillon had been drinking, broke out. At the declaration of war, Marie plunged herself into fund-raising for the War Effort, yet even this great patriotic duty went unrecognized for she was never invited to star in any Royal Command Performances – the organizing committees still considered her morally 'gauche'. All this time the rows between Dillon and herself were becoming more and more violent, until, to avoid Dillon's brutal attacks, she was granted a separation in 1920.

The last years of her life were dedicated to her audiences – she seemed to perform automatically for as her strength ebbed, and alcohol took over, she would be incoherent and oblivious of anything and anyone off-stage, but as soon as her music cue was played, she 'switched on' her old personality for her audience. Her last appearance was on 4 October 1922 at Edmonton where she collapsed on stage – dying three days later. So great was her popularity and esteem that after the funeral, 100 000 people filed past her grave. The songs she bequeathed to posterity were 'Oh! Mr Porter', 'One of the ruins Cromwell knocked about a bit' and 'Don't dilly dally'.

'Buy me some almond rock' contains a somewhat shady lyric full of innuendo of which the title is open to many connotations. The melody has a jaunty character that only Marie could compliment and the chorus, although rarely heard these days, deserves better airing. Note the references to Gladstone's cabinet, especially Labouchere (with hidden reference to his 'Homosexual Bill') and Randolph Churchill in the chorus, and the now-familiar figure of a disgraced Sir Charles Dilke in verse three. H. G. Banks' cover designs had by now reached a pinnacle in their ornamentation, but here his innocent cameo of Marie, eye-catching in its intrinsic beauty, seems strangely unconnected in style with the remainder of the cover.

Oh! Mr Porter – Published 1893
Perhaps the most well-known of Marie Lloyd's songs, 'Oh! Mr Porter' is regretably only heard today in chorus form. One can imagine Marie's 'business' when performing this song, especially on lines such as 'But my old friend grasped my leg and pulled me back again' – there seems plenty of scope for many double meanings. Significantly the whole of the chorus lyric may sound dubious when compared with two other songs that Marie sang – both about country girls visiting London and their experiences – 'I've never lost my last train yet' and 'What did she know about railways' which includes the line 'She'd never had her ticket punched before'.

So her Sister says – Published 16 January 1894
Jenny Valmore was one of those music hall stalwarts who, although never acquiring big star status, was on many bills throughout the country for over twenty years. 'So her sister says' is one of the many George Le Brunn compositions which may still be heard occasionally today: the lyrics by J. P. Harrington tell of the gossip directed at Mary Ann, the new neighbour – a well-observed piece of descriptive writing so true to life. The last three lines of the chorus express the views of the nosiest curtain-twitcher of them all which put an entirely different complexion on Mary Ann's social life.

Catch 'Em Alive Oh! – Published 1894
Gus Elen (1863–1940) on the stage characterized cockney tragi-comedy at its best and most of his songs emphasized it – 'It's a great big shame', ''Alf pint of ale' and 'The 'ouses in between'. He came to fame in 1891 as a coster comedian and his stage personality was typified by his dead-pan face tinged with a streak of world-weariness which could raise a laugh or a tear in a short space of time. When gramophone records were introduced, Elen was invited to record a song in front of a microphone. However, because of his ingrained stage technique of jogging around the stage while performing his songs (a good strategy when playing to hostile audiences), he had to be forcibly restrained in front of the microphone in order to achieve a comprehensible recording.

In the last ten years of his life, Elen retired to a cottage by the sea where he lived comfortably. He did however, make a comeback in 1932 for a Royal Variety Performance.

Arthur Seldon was not only the writer of this and many other songs, but also a popular artiste in his own right. This song of the fly-paper seller is well within the compass of Elen's dead-pan humour – the melody is simply a vehicle for the lyrics – nothing more, but the lyrics manage to include not only a few outrageous puns, pokes at bald-headed men, but also a tilt at Gladstone and his Irish Home Rule Bill!

That Gorgonzola Cheese – Published 1894

Food songs seemed to be one of Harry Champion's stock-in-trade. Born in 1866, he first appeared at the 'Queens' Poplar as a black-faced comedian using the name 'Will Conway'. His paunchy round face and his rough vigour assisted in his promotion of those long-standing favourites that he originated – 'Any old iron', 'I'm Henery the eighth' and 'Boiled beef and carrots'. He was a favourite on the halls right into the twenties and with the advent of radio, he was heard throughout the nation. He died at the age of seventy-six and was sorely missed by his devoted public.

Harry Champion's melody line to 'That gorgonzola cheese' was of his own inimitable style and the lyrics by Fred Leigh give a hilariously lurid account as to the long (and strong) shelf-life of this particular piece of cheese. H. G. Banks' cover has here attained an artistry that no other illustrator of his time could equal – he even develops the story line with the witty explanatory headings to his cameos.

Slight Mistake on the Part of my Valet – Published 1897

George Robey was born in 1869 and started his career in music hall at the Oxford in 1891: his trade-marks were his thick eyebrows and clergyman's coat – props that made him a successful prospect in pantomime, revue and music hall, where he became known as 'The Prime Minister of Mirth'. His character studies such as 'The Prehistoric Man' and 'Oliver Cromwell' became famous throughout the halls up and down the country while his extraordinary patter sometimes was longer in duration than the song which it accompanied. Robey married twice and in the First World War he toured army units at the front and made fund-raising concerts for which he was officially recognized in 1918 with the award of a CBE (he was offered a knighthood at the time but he refused it because he thought it would injure his stage image). In 1916 he was cast in the revue 'The Bing Boys Are Here' and during one sketch, he sang the song that was to become world-famous – 'If you were the only girl in the world'. After the war George Robey took up various roles in straight plays and in 1935 he played Falstaff in a production of *Henry IV* at His Majesty's Theatre – ten years later he played the dying Falstaff in Lawrence Olivier's film *Henry V*.

In February 1954 his career was crowned when he received a knighthood, yet sadly he died only nine months later.

Although the melody of 'Slight mistake on the part of my valet' is not of the 'first water', the lyrics compensate with gems of situation comedy bordering on French farce – it seems strange however, for one of Robey's songs not to include any patter.

The Bobbies of the Queen – Published 1897

There were many artistes who, over the years, toured the halls the length and breadth of the country, yet who never made any lasting name for themselves – Maud Santley was one such. With her song 'The Bobbies of the Queen' however, she temporarily caught the attention of the general public in 1897. The song, although written about the police force, was a side-swipe at authority during a period which saw an upsurge in nationalistic feeling caused by the outbreak of the Boer War – it was no coincidence that Leslie Stuart's song

'The Soldiers of the Queen', written fifteen years previously, was undergoing a dramatic reprise in theatres, pubs and drawing-rooms.

'The Bobbies of the Queen' however, played upon the popularity of Leslie Stuart's song to become a 'hit' of its day – it even 'borrowed' a bar and a half of his melody line in its chorus!

The local bobby had been a figure of popular fun ever since the police force was established sixty years earlier, and although most of the lyrics are harmless in their satire, the song was nevertheless immensely successful and applauded by the audiences where it was performed, but frowned upon the the Establishment.

On the day King Edward gets his Crown on – Published 1902

The decades of prim Victorian rule and the seemingly never-ending war in South Africa made the British public yearn for 'something different' – a difference symbolized by the jovial personage of the future Edward VII. These aspirations were summed up in 'On the day King Edward gets his Crown on' – the impending death of Queen Victoria could not come quickly enough for her subjects at the beginning of a gay, hurly-burly era where she seemed totally out of place. Harry Pleon, a comedian-artiste and songwriter, although short of stature, had found a 'greatness' in the public's affections only eclipsed by that of 'Little Tich'. Pleon's unchallenged tilt at royalty in this song demonstrates that he deeply understood the innermost desires of his fellow-countrymen and by his innocent, yet subtle use of humour, he realized his role as the voice of his audiences.

Every event heralded by 'The day King Edward gets his Crown on' builds into the lyrics an air of expectancy for the 'good times' that were to come – 'Father's going to change his socks and Auntie have a bath' – and the sentiments echoed by the chorus clearly predict the splendour of the Edwardian era that was just around the corner.

An Old Man's Darling – Published 1903

Vesta Victoria was born in 1874 – daughter of Joe Lawrence who was the manager of the Cardiff Empire. Vesta became involved at an early age with music hall and with her talent, charm and pretty face, soon claimed her first success with 'Daddy wouldn't buy me a bow-wow' from which she never looked back. There are many comparisons between Vesta and Marie Lloyd – her stage act was similar although more subdued in certain 'moral' aspects – they both were in the forefront of the VAF strike in 1907.

In later years Vesta created new songs which have remained as fresh as when they were first written – 'Waiting at the church' and 'It's all right in the summertime'. On the 'boards' for most of her life, a constant favourite with her audiences, Vesta died in 1951.

There have been many songs, in both folk and 'pop' music, discouraging marriage with an old man, so 'An old man's darling' comes as a breath of fresh air, expounding as it does the advantages of such a union – the old man's constant attention to his young wife, probably brought about by his concern at the possibility of her flirtations with younger men, even though the lyrics state 'They're not jealous like the young men, no! For they will trust you anywhere you go'.

5. ENCORE!

The following two works are music hall songs which have never been published before. In the process of preparing this book, I had been researching in the Ascherberg Archives – some of which had not been sorted or catalogued for over fifty years. On the afternoon of 30 October 1975, I was accompanied by Mr Peter Honri, who was himself collecting data for his book *The Lion Comiques:* as we were browsing through the many piles of Hopwood & Crew file copies of music hall songs, we came across these works in proof form, complete with the blue pencilled corrections. Our excitement turned to astonishment however, when upon examining 'She's so sweet (Sweet Sweet Sweet)' we further discovered a Concanen sketch on greased paper as though awaiting immediate delivery to the lithographic printers. This astutely-drawn cover sketch is reproduced here without any embellishment and shows how Concanen's sketches provided rough guidelines for the calligraphy which was added later. It is obvious that at this proof stage no one had decided upon the correct title – the cover sketch giving 'Sweet Sweet Sweet' and the music proof stating 'She's so sweet'.

The Stock Number (i.e. the Hopwood & Crew plate number) given on the proof copy of this song is H & C 2451: having thoroughly and carefully checked the British Museum and Stationers' Hall, it was found that no form of this work had been published and that the work logged in the Hopwood & Crew Stock Book under H & C 2451 was in fact 'Is the guv'nor in?' published in 1883. From this the probable year of composition can be deduced for this unpublished work as all Stock Numbers at least from 1875 onwards run chronologically. In addition, the artiste mentioned on the unpublished work is G. H. Macdermott, who also performed 'Is the guv'nor in?' and in all probability he decided at the last moment that 'Sweet Sweet Sweet' was not as strong a contender for his stage act as 'Is the guv'nor in?' – the former being dropped before it came to print and the latter substituted.

'Sweet Sweet Sweet' has no strong melody line – only a progression of musical phrases loosely held together by a banal chorus after a modulation of key. The lyrics provide an insight into the everyday pastimes and haunts of the 1880s 'jet set'.

'Beautiful Dora' by 'Jingo' Hunt dates from around 1875 and is mentioned in the Hopwood & Crew Stock Book but without any note of publication date, quantities or plate detail. From my researches it has been established that this song had progressed no further than the 'proofing' stage. One can only surmise that this song might have been destined for either Leybourne, with whom Hunt worked closely at the time the song was written, or Macdermott, who about that time became a regular purveyor of Hunt's songs – the truth of the matter will never be known.

Hunt's lyrical melodies have many similarities in style with those that Sullivan wrote for his comic operas; 'Beautiful Dora' is so tuneful a pastoral love song that it is quite unfathomable why it was never published – its melody alone would have been enough to start an audience humming and whistling for weeks on end – so powerful yet so simple is its lilt. The melody's structure is an ABA form with the B section being a modulation to the dominant key – this concept would have made the whole suitable for a barrel-organ, for it does not take much imagination to hear those jangling tones emanating from the accompaniment. (Apart from the corrections already pencilled in on the 'proof' copy, the Gs in bars 29 and 37 of the song ought to be sharpened.)

As seeds that have lain dormant in the dark corners of time, we now hope that these songs will have a belated chance to flourish in the gentle light of the new interest in, and enthusiasm for, the British music hall.

Beautiful Dora.

WRITTEN AND COMPOSED BY

G. W. HUNT.

VOICE.

TEMPO DI VALSE.

PIANO.

f

H & C. 1668.

Some may be craz'd with wild ad - mi - ra - tion,
O - ver a pic - ture, a pet, or a pearl,
What - eer can cause a sweet - er sen - sa - tion,
Than that sweet pic - ture - a fair En - glish Girl!

Down a-mongst ver---dant trees and bow-ers,
Dwells the dear one I think oh! so fair,
While she flits to and fro midst the flowers, The
sun likes to play with her gold---en hair.

CHORUS.

Beau_ti_ful Do - - ra, O! if you saw her! Feeding the
chicks who come to her call, Beau_ti_ful Do - - ra,
how I a_dore her, Beau_ti_ful Do- - - ra, fair est of
all.
f

1

Some may go crazed with wild admiration,
Over a picture, a pet, or a pearl,
Whate'er can cause a sweeter sensation,
Than that picture, a fair English girl!
Down amongst verdant trees and bowers,
Dwells the dear one, I think oh! so fair!
While she flits to and fro midst the flowers,
The sun likes to play with her golden hair!

CHORUS.

Beautiful Dora, O if you saw her!
Feeding the chicks who come to her call,
Beautiful Dora, how I adore her,
Beautiful Dora, fairest of all!

2

O those blest chicks! and happy chich mother,
Sometimes to be one I think I'd rejoice,
How they come tumbling over each other,
Whene'er they hear sweet Dora's voice;
Her Dad he's a jovial English farmer,
Britons alone with such daughters are blest,
His face glows with pride as he'll gaze on my charmer,
Red as the sun when he's sinking to rest.

CHORUS.

3

The Butterfly hovers about her fair tresses,
The Rose seems to bow whene'er goes by,
As though 'twere eclipsed and silent, confesses,
While the Lark seems to sing for her up in the sky;
None of your dainty vain-smitten misses,
Cheeks like the ripe peach, blooming with health,
Lips that were made for sweetest kisses,
Hair that rolls down in its golden wealth.

CHORUS.

4

What would I give to be the possesor,
Of one so innocent, winsome and fair,
Happy the one whoe'er may caress her,
For such a jewel is priceless and rare;
But she'll not leave her dear old Dad,
Lonely to baffle in age with life's stream,
So she'll send others lovingly mad,
As this one who of her's content to dream.

CHORUS.

SWEET SWEET
CAFÉ RESTAURANT
SONG BY
MACDERMOTT
Composed by
London

SHE'S SO SWEET.

Written by
G. H. MACDERMOTT.

Arranged by
ERNEST J. SYMONS.

H & C. 2451.

I know the sweet_est girl in Town, Sirs, Quite the sweet_est of the
sweet, And tho' to ev'_ _ry move she's down, Sirs, Just the
sort of girl you'd eat, I see my An_ _gel ev'_ _ry
morn_ing, Meet my Se_ _raph ev'_ _ry day, Ar_cade and

Re_gent Street a_-dorn_ing, At night the Mu_-sic Hall or
CHORUS.
play, And here's the cry, as she goes by, The Dudes and
p
Chap_pies glass in eye, By Jove she's grand, that waist, those
feet, And what a hand, oh! aint she sweet!

Tempo di Polka.
H. I. J. K. L. M. N. oh! aint she sweet! She's so sweet, sweet,
sweet! She's so sweet, sweet, sweet! H. I. J. K. L. M. N. oh!
aint she sweet! I could kiss her toe, She's so sweet, sweet,
sweet!
ff

1

I know the sweetest girl in town, Sirs,
Quite the sweetest of the sweet,
And tho' to every move she's down, Sirs,
Just the sort of girl you'd eat;
I see my angel every morning,
Meet my seraph every day,
Arcade and Regent Street adorning,
At night the Music Hall or play.

CHORUS.

And here's the cry as she goes by,
The Dudes and Chap-pies, Glass in eye,
By Jove, she's grand, that waist, those feet,
And what a hand, oh! aint she sweet,
H. I. J. K. L. M. N. Oh, aint she sweet!
She's so sweet, sweet, sweet!
She's so sweet, sweet, sweet!
H. I. J. K. L. M. N. Oh, aint she sweet!
I could kiss her toe,
She's so sweet, sweet, sweet!

2

She'll breakfast at the Continental,
At the Cafe Royal she'll dine,
With just a biscuit incidental,
And a bottle or two of sparkling wine;
She "Races" too at lovely "Sandown,"
Acts at Gaiety Matinees,
And the way she takes each man down,
Really is beyond all praise.
(*Chorus.*) And here's the cry, &c.

3

She'll Breakfast at the Continental,
At the Cafe Royal she'll dine,
With just a biscuit incidental,
And a bottle or two of sparkling wine;
Others slyly whisper "Brompton."
"Chelsea," "Pimlico," so good!
One chap says she's Carrie Compton,
Of 15 South Bank, St. John's Wood.

CHORUS.

And here's the cry as she goes by,
The Dudes and Chap-pies, Glass in eye,
By Jove, she's grand, that waist, those feet,
And what a hand, oh, aint she sweet!
H. I. J. K. L. M. N. Oh, aint she sweet!
She's so sweet, sweet, sweet!
She's so sweet, sweet, sweet!
H. I. J. K. L. M. N. Oh, aint she sweet!
I could kiss her toe,
She's so sweet, sweet, sweet!

4

Now p'rhaps you'd hardly think this beauty,
Who's Photos every where you'll find,
Knows well that little word called "duty,"
And to real affection is not blind;
And spite of all this envious rumour,
She lives a pure and blameless life,
And will, if I can, in the humour,
One day catch her, be my wife.
(*Chorus.*) And here's the cry, &c.